AF429418

Dedicated

To all youngsters in various challenges not able to thrive.

Author's Note:

Mastering 69 Essential Skills for Gaining Confidence and Success

Dear Reader,

In a time were we find our weakness and failure, we tend to rethink. In such moments this is what matters self-awareness, self-motivation, Self-learning which should lead to Self-Efficacy. We call it Skill Up. Be bold, be strong. Let this words encourage and help you thrive in this world.

It is our Hope this book will not only encourage but also provide confidence to be not just a Reader but a doer or become a person of Confidence and Success.

SkillUp is to help people help others. But for that some time or many time we need a holistic growth. My parents would share a prayer which was on the basis of how Jesus Grew. It encouraged me a lot and it's really true. It's a verse which says Jesus Grew in Wisdom and in stature and in favor with God and Man. Yes, all are important. I have share some of the key skills which are going crazy or it's a basic. There are 1000's of skills which can be included, but I have shared some with understanding to the sectors that are very prevalent for a private sector.

Welcome to "Mastering 69 Essential Skills and Soft Skills for Success"! As the author, I am thrilled to present this comprehensive guide aimed at helping you navigate the complex landscape of skills and soft skills crucial for personal and professional growth. Drawing upon years of research and experience, this book distils key insights, practical tips, and actionable strategies to empower you in various aspects of life. Whether you are a student, a seasoned professional, or someone embarking on a journey of self-improvement, I hope this book serves as a valuable resource on your path to success.

Remember, mastering skills and soft skills is an ongoing journey, and I encourage you to embrace each chapter with curiosity, dedication, and a willingness to learn as this is just the beginning.

Best wishes on your journey of skill mastery!

SkillUp regards,

Emrys. E

How to use this Book

Welcome to "Mastering 69 Essential Skills for Success"! This comprehensive guide is designed to help you develop and enhance a wide range of soft skills essential for personal and professional growth. Whether you're a student, a working professional, or someone looking to improve your interpersonal abilities, this book offers valuable insights, practical tips, and actionable strategies to succeed in various aspects of life. Here's how you can make the most of this book:

Explore Each Skill: Each skill is presented in a structured format, covering approx nine key points, including importance, concept, takeaway, study material/resources, activity, training guide, **Did You Know?**, PPT/e-book Guide, and video guide. Take your time to read through each section to gain a comprehensive understanding of the skill.

Choose Your Focus: You can start by exploring skills and soft skills that are most relevant to your current goals or areas for improvement. Whether you're interested in enhancing communication skills, mastering time management, or learning about event planning, feel free to navigate to the respective sections.

Refer to Ideas for Study Material/Resources: Take advantage of the recommended study materials and resources provided for each soft skill. Whether its books, online courses, or industry publications, these resources can further enhance your knowledge and understanding of the topic.

You also have various resources in the drive such as E-Books, a series of A Needy Trainers' Guide, Tool Kit, Concept notes, a Journal, Books on the Skill topics and YouTube Links (Ted Talks 5 and Tutorial Link) etc.

Some Training Ideas for Facilitation: The training guide section offers practical guidance on how to develop and improve each soft skill. From basic principles to advanced techniques, the training guide provides step-by-step instructions and tips for honing your abilities.

Discover Interesting Facts: Did you know sections offer fascinating insights and trivia related to each skill? These facts provide additional context and understanding.

The PPT/e-book and video guide sections offer visual aids and multimedia resources to supplement your learning or help people learn. Whether you prefer slideshows or video tutorials, these resources provide additional support training.
.Take Action: As you read through the book, consider how you can apply the insights and techniques to your personal or professional life. Set specific goals for improvement and take proactive steps to implement what you've learned.
We hope you find this book insightful, practical, and valuable in your journey toward mastering essential Skills and soft skills for success. Remember, continuous learning and growth are key to unlocking your full potential!

Happy reading and skill-building!

Table

Appendix- Drive Resource
- ➢ 69 Essential Soft Skills for Success EBook – Access
- ➢ Resource Google Drive - Access
- ➢ 69 Concept Note Video - Access

Skill 1: Communication

Importance:
Effective communication skills are vital in every aspect of life, from personal relationships to professional success. They allow individuals to express themselves clearly, understand others better, and navigate various social and professional situations with ease.

Concept:
Communication skills encompass verbal, non-verbal, and written forms of expression. They involve active listening, empathy, clarity of speech, body language, and the ability to convey ideas persuasively. Mastering these skills empowers individuals to connect deeply with others and convey their messages effectively.

Takeaway: Guide for Students and Professionals
By mastering communication skills, individuals can enhance their personal and professional relationships, boost their career prospects, and become more influential leaders. Effective communication fosters collaboration, reduces misunderstandings, and promotes a positive and productive environment.

For a beginner student today, mastering the concept of effective communication is crucial for success in academic, professional, and personal settings. Effective communication involves several key elements: active listening, which includes paying full attention to the speaker, understanding their message, and responding thoughtfully; clarity and conciseness, which help avoid misunderstandings by keeping the message straightforward and well-organized; and nonverbal communication, which utilizes body language, eye contact, and tone of voice to reinforce the message. Additionally, empathy and emotional intelligence are essential for understanding and sharing the feelings of others, thereby building trust and strong relationships. This includes self-awareness, self-regulation, and social skills. Feedback is another critical component, as it involves giving and receiving constructive criticism effectively to foster improvement and mutual understanding. In today's digital age, proficiency in digital communication is also necessary, encompassing email etiquette, social media interactions, and virtual meeting skills. Lastly, cultural awareness is vital in a globalized world, requiring respect for diverse perspectives and adapting communication to fit different cultural contexts. By developing these skills, students can enhance their ability to communicate clearly and effectively across various platforms and situations.

Ideas for Study Material/Resources:
Books: "How to Win Friends and Influence People" by Dale Carnegie, "Crucial Conversations" by Kerry Patterson, Joseph Grenny, Ron McMillan, and Al Switzler.
Online Courses: Platforms like Udemy, Coursera, and LinkedIn Learning offer courses on communication skills.
Articles and Blogs: Harvard Business Review, Forbes, and Psychology Today often feature articles on effective communication techniques.

Ideas for Activity:
Conduct role-playing exercises where participants practice different communication scenarios, such as delivering feedback, negotiating, or handling conflicts.

Some Training Ideas for Facilitation:
Start with the basics: understanding the elements of communication and identifying common communication barriers.
Teach active listening techniques and the importance of empathy in communication.
Provide strategies for effective verbal and non-verbal communication.
Offer opportunities for practice and feedback to reinforce learning.

Did You Know?
Studies show that up to 93% of communication is non-verbal, including body language, facial expressions, and tone of voice.
Good communication skills can increase job prospects and earning potential, as employers often prioritize these skills in candidates.

Ideas for Presentation:
Create a PowerPoint presentation or e-book summarizing key concepts, tips, and techniques for improving communication skills. Include visuals and real-life examples to enhance understanding.

Training Video Guide:
Develop video tutorials demonstrating various aspects of communication skills, such as active listening, assertiveness, and delivering presentations. Incorporate scenarios and role-plays to illustrate effective communication in action. Use role plays if necessary.

Skill 2: Time Management

Importance:
Effective time management is crucial for maximizing productivity, achieving goals, and reducing stress. It enables individuals to prioritize tasks, meet deadlines, and maintain a healthy work-life balance.

Concept:
Time management involves setting goals, planning tasks, and allocating time efficiently. It includes techniques such as prioritization, task batching, and overcoming procrastination to make the most of available time.

Takeaway: Guide for Students and Professionals
By mastering time management skills, individuals can improve their efficiency, accomplish more in less time, and experience less stress. Effective time management leads to greater productivity as you save time and also leads to a sense of accomplishment.

For a beginner student today, mastering the concept of time management is crucial for achieving success in both academic and personal endeavors. Time management involves effectively organizing and planning how to allocate time between various activities to ensure that tasks are completed efficiently and deadlines are met without unnecessary stress. Key strategies include setting clear and achievable goals, prioritizing tasks based on their importance and deadlines, creating a structured schedule or to-do list, and avoiding procrastination by breaking larger tasks into smaller, manageable steps. Additionally, it is important to allocate time for breaks and self-care to maintain overall well-being and productivity. By developing strong time management skills, students can enhance their ability to balance academic responsibilities with extracurricular activities and personal commitments, leading to a more productive and less stressful life.

Ideas for Study Material/Resources:
Books: "Getting Things Done" by David Allen, "Eat That Frog!" by Brian Tracy, "The 7 Habits of Highly Effective People" by Stephen R. Covey.
Online Courses: Platforms like Udemy, Coursera, and LinkedIn Learning offer courses on time management.
Articles and Blogs: Productivity blogs such as Lifehacker, Todoist Blog, and Zen Habits provide valuable tips and techniques for time management.

Ideas for Activity:
Conduct time-tracking exercises where participants monitor their activities for a day and identify time-wasting habits.
Teach techniques such as the Eisenhower Matrix or Pomodoro Technique through interactive workshops.

Some Training Ideas for Facilitation:
Start by helping participants identify their goals and priorities.
Teach strategies for effective goal setting, task prioritization, and creating a daily schedule.
Provide tools and resources for time management, such as calendar apps and task management software.
Offer tips for overcoming common time management challenges, such as multitasking and procrastination.

Did You Know?
Research shows that multitasking can reduce productivity by up to 40% and increase the likelihood of errors.

Ideas for Presentation:
Create a PowerPoint presentation or e-book summarizing key time management principles, techniques, and tools. Include practical examples and case studies to illustrate effective time management strategies.

Training Video Guide:
Develop video tutorials demonstrating various time management techniques, such as goal setting, task prioritization, and time blocking. Use real-life scenarios to illustrate the benefits of effective time management.

Skill 3: Problem Solving

Importance:
Effective problem-solving skills are essential for overcoming challenges, making informed decisions, and achieving goals. They enable individuals to analyze problems, generate solutions, and implement effective strategies.

Concept:
Problem-solving involves identifying issues, gathering relevant information, analyzing alternatives, and selecting the best course of action. It requires creativity, critical thinking, and adaptability to solve complex problems effectively.

Takeaway: Guide for Students and Professionals
By mastering problem-solving skills, individuals can become more resourceful, innovative, and proactive in addressing challenges. Effective problem-solving leads to better decision-making, increased confidence, and improved outcomes.

For a beginner student today, mastering the concept of problem-solving is crucial for navigating both academic challenges and real-life situations. Problem-solving involves identifying solutions to complex or challenging issues by systematically breaking them down into manageable parts, analyzing the root causes, and developing effective strategies to address them. Key steps in problem-solving include clearly defining the problem, brainstorming potential solutions, evaluating the pros and cons of each option, and selecting the most viable solution. Creativity, logical reasoning, and perseverance are essential in this process, as they enable students to think outside the box and approach problems from different angles. By developing strong problem-solving skills, students can enhance their ability to tackle obstacles confidently and effectively, leading to improved academic performance and a greater capacity to handle life's various challenges.

Ideas for Study Material/Resources:
Books: "The Art of Problem Solving" by Russell L. Ackoff, "Thinking, Fast and Slow" by Daniel Kahneman, "Problem Solving 101" by Ken Watanabe.
Online Courses: Platforms like Udemy, Coursera, and edX offer courses on problem-solving techniques.
Articles and Blogs: Websites like Medium, Harvard Business Review, and Psychology Today publish articles on problem-solving strategies and case studies.

Ideas for Activity:
Conduct problem-solving workshops where participants tackle real-life scenarios and brainstorm solutions as a group.
Utilize case studies or role-playing exercises to simulate problem-solving situations and encourage active participation.

Some Training Ideas for Facilitation:
Start by defining the problem and breaking it down into manageable components.
Teach techniques such as root cause analysis, brainstorming, and decision matrices to generate and evaluate solutions.
Provide guidance on implementing and evaluating the effectiveness of chosen solutions.
Encourage a growth mindset and resilience in the face of setbacks during the problem-solving process.

Did You Know?
Research shows that individuals with strong problem-solving skills are more likely to excel in both academic and professional settings.

Ideas for Presentation:
Create a PowerPoint presentation or e-book summarizing key problem-solving principles, techniques, and case studies. Include interactive elements to engage participants and reinforce learning.

Training Video Guide:
Develop video tutorials demonstrating various problem-solving techniques, such as SWOT analysis, fishbone diagrams, and decision trees. Use real-world examples to illustrate the application of problem-solving skills in different contexts.

Skill 4: Adaptability

Importance:
Adaptability is crucial in today's rapidly changing world, enabling individuals to thrive in unpredictable environments and embrace new opportunities. It involves being flexible, resilient, and open to change.

Concept:
Adaptability is the ability to adjust to new situations, challenges, and demands. It requires staying calm under pressure, learning from experiences, and being willing to step outside of one's comfort zone.

Takeaway: Guide for Students and Professionals
By mastering adaptability skills, individuals can navigate uncertainty with confidence, seize opportunities for growth, and overcome obstacles effectively. Adaptability fosters resilience, innovation, and continuous improvement.

For a beginner student today, mastering the concept of adaptability is crucial for thriving in an ever-changing academic and personal environment. Adaptability refers to the capacity to adjust to new conditions, challenges, or environments with a positive and flexible attitude. It involves being open to change, learning from new experiences, and being willing to modify one's approach as needed. Key aspects of adaptability include maintaining a growth mindset, which embraces challenges as opportunities for learning and development, and being resilient in the face of setbacks. Additionally, being adaptable means being able to quickly grasp new concepts and skills, as well as effectively managing stress and uncertainty. By developing strong adaptability skills, students can better navigate the dynamic nature of today's world, enhance their ability to learn and grow continuously, and improve their capacity to handle diverse situations and challenges with confidence.

Ideas for Study Material/Resources:
Books: "Mindset: The New Psychology of Success" by Carol S. Dweck, "Antifragile: Things That Gain from Disorder" by Nassim Nicholas Taleb, "The Obstacle Is the Way" by Ryan Holiday.
Online Courses: Platforms like Coursera, LinkedIn Learning, and Skillshare offer courses on resilience and adaptability.
Articles and Blogs: Websites like Psychology Today, Harvard Business Review, and Forbes often feature articles on adaptability and resilience.

Ideas for Activity:
Conduct scenario-based exercises where participants practice adapting to unexpected changes or challenges.
Encourage participants to reflect on past experiences of adapting to change and identify strategies that were effective.

Some Training Ideas for Facilitation:
Start by discussing the importance of adaptability and the benefits it brings in various aspects of life.
Teach techniques for building resilience, such as reframing challenges, practicing self-care, and seeking support from others.
Provide strategies for embracing change, including staying curious, seeking feedback, and being open to learning.

Did You Know?
Research shows that individuals with high levels of adaptability are more likely to succeed in dynamic work environments and experience greater job satisfaction.

Ideas for Presentation:
Create a PowerPoint presentation or e-book summarizing key concepts, techniques, and case studies related to adaptability. Include practical tips and exercises for building adaptability skills.

Training Video Guide:
Develop video tutorials demonstrating various adaptability techniques, such as reframing challenges, practicing mindfulness, and fostering a growth mindset. Use real-life examples to illustrate the importance of adaptability in different situations.

Skill 5: Teamwork and Collaboration

Importance:
Effective teamwork and collaboration are essential for achieving shared goals, fostering innovation, and building strong relationships. They enable individuals to work together harmoniously, leverage diverse perspectives, and maximize collective potential.

Concept:
Teamwork and collaboration involve communication, trust, and mutual respect among team members. They require active listening, empathy, and a willingness to compromise for the greater good of the team.

Takeaway: Guide for Students and Professionals
By mastering teamwork and collaboration skills, individuals can contribute effectively to team projects, resolve conflicts constructively, and create a supportive team environment. Effective teamwork leads to increased productivity, creativity, and satisfaction for all team members.

Ideas for Study Material/Resources:
Books: "The Five Dysfunctions of a Team" by Patrick Lencioni, "Crucial Conversations" by Kerry Patterson, Joseph Grenny, Ron McMillan, and Al Switzler, "Collaborative Intelligence" by Dawna Markova and Angie McArthur.
Online Courses: Platforms like Coursera, edX, and LinkedIn Learning offer courses on teamwork and collaboration skills.
Articles and Blogs: Harvard Business Review, Forbes, and Fast Company often feature articles on effective teamwork and collaboration strategies.

Ideas for Activity:
Conduct team-building exercises where participants work together to solve challenges or complete tasks.
Facilitate group discussions on effective communication, conflict resolution, and decision-making within teams.

Some Training Ideas for Facilitation:
Start by discussing the importance of teamwork and collaboration in achieving common goals.
Teach strategies for building trust, fostering open communication, and establishing clear roles and responsibilities within teams.
Provide guidance on managing conflicts, resolving differences, and promoting inclusivity within diverse teams.

Did You Know?
Research shows that teams with high levels of trust and collaboration outperform those with low levels of cohesion and cooperation.

Ideas for Presentation:
Create a PowerPoint presentation or e-book summarizing key concepts, techniques, and best practices for effective teamwork and collaboration. Include case studies and real-life examples to illustrate successful team dynamics.

Training Video Guide:
Develop video tutorials demonstrating various teamwork and collaboration techniques, such as brainstorming, consensus-building, and team decision-making processes. Use role-plays and simulations to showcase effective team interactions and problem-solving.

Skill 6: Leadership

Importance:
Effective leadership is essential for guiding teams, inspiring others, and driving organizational success. It involves vision, integrity, and the ability to motivate and empower others to achieve their full potential.

Concept:
Leadership encompasses traits such as vision, communication, decision-making, and empathy. It involves setting direction, aligning goals, and creating a supportive environment for team members to thrive.

Takeaway: Guide for Students and Professionals
By mastering leadership skills, individuals can lead with confidence, inspire trust, and influence positive change within their teams and organizations. Effective leadership fosters collaboration, innovation, and high-performance cultures.

For a beginner student today, mastering the concept of leadership is crucial for inspiring and guiding others towards achieving common goals. Leadership involves the ability to influence, motivate, and enable others to contribute to the success of their group or organization. Effective leaders communicate a clear vision, set a positive example, and foster a supportive and productive environment. Key aspects of leadership include decision-making, where leaders must evaluate options and make informed choices; accountability, where leaders take responsibility for their actions and outcomes; and empathy, which involves understanding and addressing the needs and concerns of team members. Good leaders also exhibit strong interpersonal skills, such as active listening, conflict resolution, and the ability to build trust and rapport. By developing leadership skills, students can enhance their ability to inspire and manage teams, drive projects forward, and create a positive impact in their communities and future careers.

Ideas for Study Material/Resources:
Books: "Leaders Eat Last" by Simon Sinek, "The 21 Irrefutable Laws of Leadership" by John C. Maxwell, "Dare to Lead" by Brené Brown.
Online Courses: Platforms like Coursera, Udemy, and Harvard Business School Online offer courses on leadership development.
Articles and Blogs: Forbes, Harvard Business Review, and Inc. Magazine often feature articles on leadership best practices and case studies.

Ideas for Activity:
Conduct leadership development workshops where participants engage in self-reflection and leadership exercises.
Facilitate group discussions on leadership styles, strengths, and areas for development.

Some Training Ideas for Facilitation:
Start by exploring different leadership styles and their impact on team dynamics.
Teach skills such as effective communication, decision-making, delegation, and conflict resolution.
Provide opportunities for practicing leadership skills through role-playing, simulations, and real-world challenges.

Did You Know?
Research shows that organizations with strong leadership pipelines are better equipped to navigate change and achieve long-term success.

Ideas for Presentation:
Create a PowerPoint presentation or e-book summarizing key leadership principles, models, and techniques. Include case studies and examples of successful leadership in action.

Training Video Guide:
Develop video tutorials demonstrating various leadership skills, such as giving feedback, coaching, and leading by example. Use real-life scenarios to illustrate effective leadership practices and inspire aspiring leaders.

Skill 7: Critical Thinking

Importance:
Critical thinking is essential for making informed decisions, solving complex problems, and evaluating information effectively. It involves analyzing, interpreting, and synthesizing information to form well-reasoned judgments and conclusions.

Concept:
Critical thinking encompasses skills such as logical reasoning, analysis, and evaluation. It requires curiosity, skepticism, and the ability to consider multiple perspectives before reaching a conclusion.

Takeaway: Guide for Students and Professionals
By mastering critical thinking skills, individuals can become more discerning, creative, and independent thinkers. Critical thinking enables individuals to identify biases, challenge assumptions, and make sound decisions based on evidence and reason.

For a beginner student today, mastering the concept of critical thinking is essential for navigating the complexities of the modern world and making informed decisions. Critical thinking involves the objective analysis and evaluation of information to form well-reasoned judgments or conclusions. Key components of critical thinking include questioning assumptions, examining evidence, and considering alternative perspectives. Effective critical thinkers are open-minded, curious, and able to recognize their own biases and assumptions. They use logical reasoning and evidence to support their arguments, rather than relying solely on emotions or opinions. Additionally, critical thinkers are adept at identifying and solving problems, as they can break down complex issues into manageable components and develop creative solutions. By honing their critical thinking skills, students can become more discerning consumers of information, better problem solvers, and more persuasive communicators, ultimately preparing them for success in both their academic and professional pursuits.

Ideas for Study Material/Resources:
Books: "Thinking, Fast and Slow" by Daniel Kahneman, "The Art of Thinking Clearly" by Rolf Dobelli, "Critical Thinking: An Introduction" by Alec Fisher.
Online Courses: Platforms like edX, Coursera, and FutureLearn offer courses on critical thinking skills.
Articles and Blogs: Psychology Today, Scientific American, and The Conversation often feature articles on critical thinking techniques and applications.

Ideas for Activity:
Conduct critical thinking exercises where participants analyze case studies, evaluate arguments, and solve logic puzzles.
Facilitate group discussions on logical fallacies, cognitive biases, and strategies for improving critical thinking skills.

Some Training Ideas for Facilitation:
Start by defining critical thinking and its importance in decision-making and problem-solving.
Teach techniques such as Socratic questioning, evidence evaluation, and argument analysis.
Provide opportunities for practicing critical thinking skills through real-world scenarios and thought experiments.

Did You Know?
Research shows that individuals with strong critical thinking skills are better equipped to succeed academically, professionally, and personally.

Ideas for Presentation:
Create a PowerPoint presentation or e-book summarizing key critical thinking concepts, techniques, and case studies. Include examples of logical reasoning and evidence-based decision-making.

Training Video Guide:
Develop video tutorials demonstrating various critical thinking techniques, such as problem-solving strategies, logical reasoning, and evidence evaluation. Use real-life examples to illustrate the application of critical thinking skills in different contexts.

Skill 8: Decision Making

Importance:
Effective decision-making is crucial for personal and professional success, as it impacts outcomes, resource allocation, and risk management. It involves analyzing options, considering consequences, and making informed choices based on available information and objectives.

Concept:
Decision-making encompasses processes such as problem identification, option generation, evaluation, and implementation. It requires clarity of goals, critical thinking, and consideration of ethical and moral implications.

Takeaway: Guide for Students and Professionals
By mastering decision-making skills, individuals can make better choices, mitigate risks, and achieve desired outcomes more consistently. Effective decision-making leads to increased efficiency, innovation, and organizational success.

For a beginner student today, mastering the concept of decision-making is crucial for navigating the myriad choices they encounter in academics, personal life, and future career paths. Decision-making involves the process of selecting the best course of action from among multiple alternatives. Key elements of effective decision-making include gathering relevant information, evaluating potential outcomes, considering risks and benefits, and weighing various factors before making a choice. Good decision-makers also possess strong analytical skills, intuition, and the ability to manage uncertainty. Additionally, they understand the importance of ethical considerations and are mindful of the potential impact of their decisions on themselves and others. By developing strong decision-making skills, students can enhance their ability to make informed choices, solve problems effectively, and take responsibility for the consequences of their actions. This not only leads to better academic performance but also prepares them for success in their future endeavors.

Ideas for Study Material/Resources:
Books: "Thinking, Fast and Slow" by Daniel Kahneman, "Decisive: How to Make Better Choices in Life and Work" by Chip Heath and Dan Heath, "Blink: The Power of Thinking Without Thinking" by Malcolm Gladwell.
Online Courses: Platforms like Coursera, Udemy, and LinkedIn Learning offer courses on decision-making strategies.
Articles and Blogs: Harvard Business Review, Forbes, and Inc. Magazine often feature articles on decision-making techniques and case studies.

Ideas for Activity:
Conduct decision-making simulations where participants are presented with scenarios and must make choices under time constraints.
Facilitate group discussions on decision-making styles, biases, and strategies for improving decision quality.

Some Training Ideas for Facilitation:
Start by discussing the importance of decision-making and the consequences of poor decision quality.
Teach decision-making frameworks such as SWOT analysis, cost-benefit analysis, and the rational decision-making model.
Provide guidance on managing uncertainty, considering alternatives, and seeking input from stakeholders in the decision-making process.

Did You Know?
Research shows that individuals who practice deliberate decision-making techniques tend to make better choices and experience fewer regrets.

Ideas for Presentation:
Create a PowerPoint presentation or e-book summarizing key decision-making concepts, techniques, and case studies. Include examples of effective decision-making in various contexts.

Training Video Guide:
Develop video tutorials demonstrating various decision-making frameworks and techniques. Use real-life examples to illustrate the application of decision-making skills in different scenarios.

Skill 9: Emotional Intelligence

Importance:
Emotional intelligence (EI) is essential for understanding and managing emotions, building strong relationships, and navigating social interactions effectively. It involves self-awareness, self-regulation, empathy, and interpersonal skills.

Concept:
Emotional intelligence encompasses the ability to recognize, understand, and manage one's own emotions, as well as the emotions of others. It involves being aware of how emotions influence behavior and relationships and using that awareness to make constructive choices.

Takeaway: Guide for Students and Professionals
By mastering emotional intelligence skills, individuals can enhance their communication, resolve conflicts, and lead with empathy and authenticity. Emotional intelligence fosters resilience, collaboration, and emotional well-being.

For a beginner student today, understanding and developing emotional intelligence (EI) is crucial for navigating social interactions, managing emotions, and building meaningful relationships. Emotional intelligence refers to the ability to recognize, understand, and manage one's own emotions, as well as to recognize and empathize with the emotions of others.

Key components of emotional intelligence include self-awareness, which involves recognizing and understanding one's own emotions, strengths, and weaknesses; self-regulation, which involves managing and controlling one's impulses, emotions, and reactions in various situations; and empathy, which involves understanding and sharing the feelings of others, and responding with compassion.

Additionally, emotional intelligence encompasses social skills, such as effective communication, conflict resolution, and teamwork, which are essential for building positive relationships and navigating social dynamics.

By developing emotional intelligence skills, students can improve their ability to communicate effectively, manage conflicts constructively, and build strong interpersonal connections. This not only enhances their personal well-being but also contributes to their academic success, career advancement, and overall fulfillment in life. Emotional intelligence is a critical skill set that empowers students to navigate the complexities of the human experience with empathy, resilience, and authenticity.

Ideas for Study Material/Resources:
Books: "Emotional Intelligence 2.0" by Travis Bradberry and Jean Greaves, "Daring Greatly" by Brené Brown, "Leadership: The Power of Emotional Intelligence" by Daniel Goleman.
Online Courses: Platforms like Coursera, LinkedIn Learning, and Emotional Intelligence Academy offer courses on emotional intelligence.
Articles and Blogs: Psychology Today, Forbes, and Greater Good Magazine often feature articles on emotional intelligence and its applications.

Ideas for Activity:
Conduct emotional intelligence assessments or quizzes to help participants understand their own emotional strengths and areas for improvement.
Facilitate group discussions or role-playing exercises to practice empathy, active listening, and conflict resolution.

Some Training Ideas for Facilitation:
Start by defining emotional intelligence and its components: self-awareness, self-regulation, social awareness, and relationship management.
Teach techniques for developing emotional intelligence, such as mindfulness, journaling, and constructive feedback.
Provide opportunities for practicing emotional intelligence skills in various interpersonal situations.

Did You Know?
Research shows that individuals with high emotional intelligence are more likely to experience success in their personal and professional lives, including higher job performance and stronger relationships.

Ideas for Presentation:
Create a PowerPoint presentation or e-book summarizing key emotional intelligence concepts, techniques, and case studies. Include practical exercises and self-assessment tools for participants.

Training Video Guide:
Develop video tutorials demonstrating various emotional intelligence skills, such as self-awareness exercises, conflict resolution techniques, and empathetic listening. Use real-life scenarios to illustrate the importance of emotional intelligence in different contexts.

Skill 10: Creativity and Innovation

Importance:
Creativity and innovation are essential for driving progress, solving problems, and staying competitive in today's dynamic world. They involve generating new ideas, taking calculated risks, and turning vision into reality.

Concept:
Creativity is the ability to think outside the box, generate original ideas, and approach challenges from new perspectives. Innovation involves implementing creative ideas to create value, whether through new products, services, processes, or business models.

Takeaway: Guide for Students and Professionals
By mastering creativity and innovation skills, individuals can unlock their creative potential, inspire others, and drive meaningful change. Creativity and innovation foster adaptability, resilience, and a culture of continuous improvement.
For a beginner student today, understanding and fostering creativity and innovation is essential for thriving in a rapidly changing world. Creativity is the ability to generate novel ideas, concepts, or solutions, while innovation involves implementing these ideas to create value or solve problems.

Key aspects of creativity and innovation include curiosity, which drives exploration and discovery; open-mindedness, which allows for considering diverse perspectives and unconventional approaches; and risk-taking, which involves stepping outside of one's comfort zone and embracing uncertainty.

Additionally, creativity and innovation require flexibility and adaptability, as well as the willingness to experiment, iterate, and learn from failure. Collaboration and interdisciplinary thinking also play a crucial role, as innovation often emerges from the intersection of different disciplines and perspectives.

By fostering creativity and innovation skills, students can develop the ability to think critically and problem-solve creatively, as well as to adapt to new challenges and opportunities. This not only enhances their academic performance but also prepares them to become lifelong learners and innovators who can contribute positively to their communities and the world at large.

Ideas for Study Material/Resources:
Books: "Creative Confidence" by Tom Kelley and David Kelley, "The Innovator's Dilemma" by Clayton M. Christensen, "Steal Like an Artist" by Austin Kleon.
Online Courses: Platforms like Udemy, Coursera, and Skillshare offer courses on creativity and innovation.
Articles and Blogs: Harvard Business Review, Fast Company, and TED often feature articles and talks on creativity and innovation.

Ideas for Activity:
Conduct brainstorming sessions or ideation workshops to generate creative ideas around specific challenges or opportunities.
Facilitate design thinking exercises or innovation challenges to encourage innovative thinking and problem-solving.

Some Training Ideas for Facilitation:
Start by exploring the principles of creativity and innovation and their importance in driving organizational success.
Teach techniques for enhancing creativity, such as mind mapping, lateral thinking, and reframing problems.
Provide guidance on fostering a culture of innovation, including encouraging experimentation, embracing failure, and celebrating success.

Did You Know?
Research shows that organizations that prioritize creativity and innovation are more likely to outperform their competitors and achieve long-term success.

Ideas for Presentation:
Create a PowerPoint presentation or e-book summarizing key creativity and innovation concepts, techniques, and case studies. Include exercises and prompts to stimulate creative thinking.

Training Video Guide:
Develop video tutorials demonstrating various creativity and innovation techniques, such as design thinking workshops, ideation exercises, and prototyping. Use real-life examples to illustrate successful innovation initiatives.

Skill 11: Organizational Skills

Importance:
Organizational skills are essential for managing time, resources, and tasks effectively. They involve prioritization, planning, and attention to detail, which are critical for achieving goals and maintaining productivity.

Concept:
Organizational skills encompass the ability to structure and manage tasks, projects, and responsibilities efficiently. They involve setting goals, creating schedules, and implementing systems to streamline workflows.

Takeaway: Guide for Students and Professionals
By mastering organizational skills, individuals can enhance their efficiency, reduce stress, and meet deadlines consistently. Organizational skills foster accountability, discipline, and a sense of control over one's work and life.

For a beginner student today, mastering organizational skills is essential for effectively managing academic workload, personal responsibilities, and extracurricular activities. Organizational skills encompass a range of abilities that facilitate efficient planning, prioritization, and execution of tasks.

Key components of organizational skills include time management, which involves allocating time wisely to various activities, setting deadlines, and creating schedules or to-do lists to stay on track. Prioritization is also important, as it enables students to identify and focus on tasks that are most important or urgent, while delegating or postponing less critical tasks.

Effective organization also involves maintaining clear and organized workspaces, both physical and digital, to minimize distractions and facilitate productivity. This includes organizing notes, files, and materials in a way that is easily accessible and manageable.

Additionally, communication skills play a crucial role in organizational effectiveness, as clear and timely communication with peers, instructors, and colleagues ensures that everyone is on the same page and working towards common goals.

By developing strong organizational skills, students can enhance their ability to manage their time efficiently, stay focused and productive, and reduce stress and overwhelm. This not only leads to improved academic performance but also fosters a sense of confidence, autonomy, and control over one's life. Organizational skills are foundational for success in both academic and professional settings, as well as in personal endeavors.

Ideas for Study Material/Resources:
Books: "Getting Things Done" by David Allen, "The 7 Habits of Highly Effective People" by Stephen R. Covey, "Eat That Frog!" by Brian Tracy.

Online Courses: Platforms like LinkedIn Learning, Skillshare, and MasterClass offer courses on time management and organization.
Articles and Blogs: Lifehacker, Forbes, and The Muse often feature articles on organization techniques and productivity hacks.

Ideas for Activity:
Conduct time management workshops or task prioritization exercises to help participants develop organizational habits.
Share tools and techniques for creating to-do lists, setting SMART goals, and managing calendars effectively.

Some Training Ideas for Facilitation:
Start by discussing the importance of organizational skills in personal and professional success.
Teach strategies for prioritizing tasks, managing distractions, and breaking down projects into manageable steps.
Provide guidance on creating effective systems for organizing information, files, and documents.

Did You Know?
Research shows that individuals with strong organizational skills are more likely to achieve their goals and experience higher levels of job satisfaction.

Ideas for Presentation:
Create a PowerPoint presentation or e-book summarizing key organizational principles, techniques, and best practices. Include templates and tools for participants to apply in their own lives.

Training Video Guide:
Develop video tutorials demonstrating various organizational techniques, such as time blocking, task batching, and using productivity apps. Use real-life examples to illustrate the benefits of effective organization.

Skill 12: Resilience

Importance:
Resilience is essential for bouncing back from setbacks, adapting to change, and overcoming adversity. It involves coping skills, optimism, and the ability to thrive in challenging situations.

Concept:
Resilience encompasses mental toughness, emotional strength, and the ability to persevere in the face of adversity. It involves reframing setbacks as opportunities for growth, building support networks, and maintaining a positive outlook.

Takeaway: Guide for Students and Professionals
By mastering resilience skills, individuals can navigate life's challenges with resilience, maintain their well-being, and achieve long-term success. Resilience fosters adaptability, perseverance, and a sense of purpose.

For a beginner student today, understanding and cultivating resilience is essential for navigating the challenges and setbacks that inevitably arise in academic, personal, and professional life. Resilience refers to the ability to bounce back from adversity, overcome obstacles, and adapt to change with strength and perseverance.

Key components of resilience include self-awareness, which involves recognizing and understanding one's own strengths, weaknesses, and emotions; optimism, which involves maintaining a positive outlook and belief in one's ability to overcome difficulties; and flexibility, which involves being open to change and willing to adapt to new circumstances.

Additionally, resilience involves developing coping strategies to manage stress and maintain well-being, such as practicing self-care, seeking social support, and reframing negative thinking patterns. It also involves learning from failure and setbacks, and using them as opportunities for growth and self-improvement.

By cultivating resilience, students can develop the ability to bounce back from setbacks stronger and more resilient than before. This not only helps them to persevere through academic challenges and achieve their goals, but also prepares them to navigate the ups and downs of life with courage, resilience, and grace. Resilience is a valuable skill that empowers students to thrive in the face of adversity and emerge stronger and more resilient than before.

Ideas for Study Material/Resources:
Books: "Option B: Facing Adversity, Building Resilience, and Finding Joy" by Sheryl Sandberg and Adam Grant, "The Resilience Factor" by Karen Reivich and Andrew Shatte, "The Obstacle Is the Way" by Ryan Holiday.
Online Courses: Platforms like Coursera, Udemy, and The Great Courses offer courses on resilience and mental well-being.
Articles and Blogs: Psychology Today, Greater Good Magazine, and Verywell Mind often feature articles on resilience-building strategies.

Ideas for Activity:
Conduct resilience-building workshops where participants share personal stories of overcoming challenges and discuss resilience strategies.
Facilitate mindfulness exercises or stress management techniques to help participants develop resilience skills.

Some Training Ideas for Facilitation:
Start by defining resilience and its importance in navigating adversity and building mental toughness.
Teach techniques for enhancing resilience, such as positive self-talk, problem-solving skills, and seeking support from others.

Provide guidance on building resilience through practices such as mindfulness, gratitude, and self-care.

Did You Know?
Research shows that individuals who develop resilience skills are better equipped to cope with stress, adapt to change, and achieve their goals.

Ideas for Presentation:
Create a PowerPoint presentation or e-book summarizing key resilience concepts, techniques, and case studies. Include practical exercises and self-assessment tools for participants.

Training Video Guide:
Develop video tutorials demonstrating various resilience-building techniques, such as mindfulness practices, cognitive restructuring, and relaxation exercises. Use real-life examples to illustrate the importance of resilience in overcoming challenges.

Skill 13: Stress Management

Importance:
Stress management is essential for maintaining well-being, productivity, and overall quality of life. It involves techniques and strategies for coping with stressors effectively and maintaining a healthy balance between work and personal life.

Concept:
Stress management encompasses awareness of stressors, identifying coping mechanisms, and implementing strategies to reduce stress levels. It involves relaxation techniques, time management, and self-care practices.

Takeaway: Guide for Students and Professionals
By mastering stress management skills, individuals can improve their resilience, mental health, and overall performance. Effective stress management leads to increased productivity, better decision-making, and enhanced overall well-being.

For a beginner student today, mastering stress management is essential for maintaining mental and physical well-being amidst the demands of academic life, personal responsibilities, and extracurricular activities. Stress management involves adopting strategies to cope with and reduce the negative effects of stress, while promoting resilience and overall health.

Key components of stress management include self-awareness, which involves recognizing signs of stress and understanding its triggers; time management, which involves prioritizing tasks, setting realistic goals, and creating schedules to avoid feeling overwhelmed; and relaxation techniques, such as deep breathing, meditation, or mindfulness, which help to calm the mind and body and reduce stress levels.

Additionally, maintaining a healthy lifestyle through regular exercise, nutritious eating, and adequate sleep is essential for managing stress and promoting overall well-being. Setting boundaries and learning to say no to excessive commitments can also help prevent burnout and reduce stress levels.

Social support is another important aspect of stress management, as talking to friends, family, or counselors about one's feelings and experiences can provide comfort, perspective, and practical advice for coping with stress.

By developing effective stress management skills, students can improve their ability to handle academic pressures, maintain balance in their lives, and thrive in the face of challenges. This not only enhances their academic performance and personal well-being, but also equips them with valuable life skills that will serve them well in the future. Stress management is a crucial skill that empowers students to take control of their lives and achieve success with resilience and grace.

Ideas for Study Material/Resources:
Books: "The Relaxation and Stress Reduction Workbook" by Martha Davis, Elizabeth Robbins Eshelman, and Matthew McKay, "Why Zebras Don't Get Ulcers" by Robert M. Sapolsky, "The Stress-Proof Brain" by Melanie Greenberg.
Online Courses: Platforms like Coursera, Udemy, and Headspace offer courses on stress management and mindfulness.
Articles and Blogs: Healthline, Mayo Clinic, and Verywell Mind often feature articles on stress management techniques and coping strategies.

Ideas for Activity:
Conduct stress management workshops where participants learn and practice relaxation techniques such as deep breathing, progressive muscle relaxation, or mindfulness meditation.
Facilitate group discussions on identifying stress triggers, developing coping strategies, and fostering a healthy work-life balance.

Some Training Ideas for Facilitation:
Start by discussing the physiological and psychological effects of stress on the body and mind.
Teach stress management techniques such as time management, setting boundaries, and practicing self-care activities.
Provide guidance on creating a supportive environment for managing stress, including fostering open communication and promoting a culture of well-being.

Did You Know?
Research shows that chronic stress can lead to a range of health problems, including anxiety, depression, and cardiovascular diseases.

Ideas for Presentation:
Create a PowerPoint presentation or e-book summarizing key stress management concepts, techniques, and tips. Include practical exercises and worksheets for participants to use in their daily lives.

Training Video Guide:
Develop video tutorials demonstrating various stress management techniques, such as guided imagery, journaling, and relaxation exercises. Use real-life scenarios to illustrate the benefits of stress management in improving overall well-being.

Skill 14: Negotiation Skills

Importance:
Negotiation skills are essential for resolving conflicts, reaching agreements, and achieving mutually beneficial outcomes in various contexts, including business, personal relationships, and everyday interactions.

Concept:
Negotiation involves communication, persuasion, and compromise to reach a satisfactory resolution for all parties involved. It requires active listening, problem-solving, and strategic thinking to achieve desired outcomes.

Takeaway: Guide for Students and Professionals
By mastering negotiation skills, individuals can build stronger relationships, resolve disputes effectively, and create win-win solutions. Effective negotiation leads to improved communication, trust, and cooperation among parties.
For a beginner student today, mastering negotiation skills is essential for navigating various situations in both academic and personal life, from resolving conflicts to reaching mutually beneficial agreements. Negotiation skills involve the ability to communicate effectively, listen actively, and collaborate with others to achieve common goals while also advocating for one's own interests.

Key components of negotiation skills include preparation, which involves researching the issue at hand, identifying goals and priorities, and anticipating potential objections or concerns. Active listening is also crucial, as it allows negotiators to understand the perspectives and interests of all parties involved, fostering empathy and rapport.

Additionally, effective communication is essential for conveying one's own needs and interests clearly and persuasively, while also being open to compromise and finding creative solutions that satisfy everyone involved. Building trust and rapport through respectful and transparent communication can also facilitate successful negotiations.

Negotiation skills also require emotional intelligence, as negotiators must be able to manage their own emotions and respond appropriately to the emotions of others, remaining calm and focused under pressure.

By developing strong negotiation skills, students can improve their ability to resolve conflicts, advocate for themselves and others, and reach mutually beneficial agreements that promote cooperation and collaboration. This not only enhances their interpersonal relationships and leadership abilities, but also prepares them for success in their future careers and endeavors. Negotiation skills are a valuable asset that empowers students to navigate complex situations with confidence and effectiveness.

Ideas for Study Material/Resources:
Books: "Getting to Yes: Negotiating Agreement Without Giving In" by Roger Fisher, William Ury, and Bruce Patton, "Never Split the Difference" by Chris Voss, "The Art of Negotiation" by Michael Wheeler.
Online Courses: Platforms like Coursera, LinkedIn Learning, and MasterClass offer courses on negotiation skills.
Articles and Blogs: Harvard Business Review, Forbes, and Negotiation Journal often feature articles on negotiation strategies and case studies.

Ideas for Activity:
Conduct negotiation role-playing exercises where participants practice different negotiation scenarios, such as salary negotiations, business deals, or conflict resolution.
Facilitate group discussions on negotiation tactics, power dynamics, and ethical considerations in negotiations.

Some Training Ideas for Facilitation:
Start by defining negotiation and its importance in various personal and professional contexts.
Teach negotiation techniques such as BATNA (Best Alternative to a Negotiated Agreement), anchoring, and framing.
Provide guidance on effective communication, active listening, and building rapport to enhance negotiation outcomes.

Did You Know?
Research shows that skilled negotiators are more likely to achieve favorable outcomes and maintain long-term relationships with their counterparts.

Ideas for Presentation:
Create a PowerPoint presentation or e-book summarizing key negotiation concepts, strategies, and case studies. Include tips and tactics for preparing for and conducting successful negotiations.

Training Video Guide:
Develop video tutorials demonstrating various negotiation techniques, such as role-playing negotiations, handling objections, and reaching win-win agreements. Use real-life scenarios to illustrate effective negotiation practices.

Skill 15: Presentation Skills (e.g., PowerPoint)

Importance:
Presentation skills are crucial for effectively conveying ideas, information, and messages to an audience. Whether in a professional setting or personal context, strong presentation skills can enhance communication and engagement.

Concept:
Presentation skills encompass the ability to organize content, deliver information clearly and persuasively, and engage the audience effectively. They involve elements such as structuring slides, using visuals, and delivering confident speeches.

Takeaway: Guide for Students and Professionals
By mastering presentation skills, individuals can deliver impactful and memorable presentations that inform, persuade, and inspire their audience. Effective presentations can lead to increased credibility, engagement, and influence.
For a beginner student today, mastering presentation skills, including the effective use of PowerPoint or other presentation tools, is essential for communicating ideas clearly and persuasively in academic, professional, and personal settings. Presentation skills encompass various aspects, including content development, design, delivery, and audience engagement.

Firstly, content development involves organizing information in a logical and engaging manner, ensuring clarity and relevance to the audience. This includes defining key messages, structuring the presentation with an introduction, body, and conclusion, and supporting points with evidence or visuals.

Design plays a crucial role in capturing the audience's attention and enhancing comprehension. Students should utilize visual aids, such as PowerPoint slides, to complement their spoken words with images, graphs, charts, and bullet points that reinforce key points and facilitate understanding. It's important to keep slides visually appealing yet uncluttered, using consistent formatting and appropriate fonts and colors.

Delivery involves effective verbal and nonverbal communication. Students should practice speaking clearly and confidently, using a conversational tone and appropriate pace. Eye contact, gestures, and body language should convey confidence and engagement. Additionally, students should be prepared to answer questions and address feedback from the audience.

Audience engagement is key to a successful presentation. Students can encourage interaction by asking questions, incorporating interactive elements like polls or quizzes, and inviting discussion. They should also be attentive to the audience's reactions and adjust their delivery accordingly.

By mastering presentation skills, students can effectively communicate their ideas, engage their audience, and leave a lasting impression. These skills are valuable not only for academic presentations but also for professional presentations, job interviews, and public speaking opportunities. With practice and feedback, students can develop confidence and competence in delivering impactful presentations that showcase their knowledge and abilities.

Ideas for Study Material/Resources:
Books: "Presentation Zen" by Garr Reynolds, "Talk Like TED: The 9 Public-Speaking Secrets of the World's Top Minds" by Carmine Gallo, "Slide:ology: The Art and Science of Creating Great Presentations" by Nancy Duarte.
Online Courses: Platforms like LinkedIn Learning, Udemy, and Skillshare offer courses on presentation skills and public speaking.
Articles and Blogs: Toastmasters International, TED Blog, and Presentation Guru often feature articles on presentation tips and techniques.

Ideas for Activity:
Conduct presentation workshops where participants practice delivering presentations on various topics and receive constructive feedback from peers.
Facilitate exercises on designing effective slides, using storytelling techniques, and managing stage fright.

Some Training Ideas for Facilitation:
Start by discussing the key components of effective presentations, including content, delivery, and audience engagement.
Teach techniques for structuring presentations, creating visually appealing slides, and delivering speeches with confidence.
Provide guidance on practicing presentations, receiving feedback, and continuously improving presentation skills.

Did You Know?
Research shows that individuals who deliver engaging presentations are more likely to capture and retain the attention of their audience and convey their message effectively.

Ideas for Presentation:
Create a PowerPoint presentation or e-book summarizing key presentation concepts, design principles, and delivery tips. Include examples of effective and ineffective presentations to illustrate best practices.

Training Video Guide:
Develop video tutorials demonstrating various presentation techniques, such as slide design, speech delivery, and audience interaction. Use real-life examples to illustrate effective presentation strategies.

Skill 16: Analytical Skills

Importance:
Analytical skills are essential for gathering, interpreting, and evaluating data to make informed decisions and solve problems effectively. They involve critical thinking, problem-solving, and attention to detail.

Concept:
Analytical skills encompass the ability to identify patterns, draw conclusions, and make recommendations based on data and evidence. They involve quantitative analysis, logical reasoning, and the ability to think systematically.

Takeaway: Guide for Students and Professionals
By mastering analytical skills, individuals can improve their decision-making abilities, identify opportunities for improvement, and solve complex problems with confidence. Analytical skills are valuable in a wide range of fields, from business and finance to science and engineering.

For a beginner student today, developing strong analytical skills is crucial for effectively understanding and evaluating complex information, making informed decisions, and solving problems. Analytical skills involve the ability to collect, process, and interpret data to draw meaningful conclusions and make logical decisions.

Key components of analytical skills include critical thinking, which involves questioning assumptions, evaluating evidence, and considering various perspectives; data analysis, which involves collecting and examining data to identify patterns, trends, and relationships; and problem-solving, which involves breaking down complex issues into manageable parts and developing effective solutions.

Additionally, students should practice logical reasoning, which involves making connections between different pieces of information and drawing reasoned conclusions. This also includes the ability to identify relevant information, filter out noise, and focus on key insights that drive understanding and decision making.

Effective communication is also a part of analytical skills, as students must be able to clearly convey their findings and recommendations through written reports, presentations, or discussions. Visual tools such as charts, graphs, and diagrams can help illustrate data and support arguments.

By developing strong analytical skills, students can enhance their ability to tackle academic challenges, conduct research, and make well-informed decisions. These skills are highly valued in various fields, including science, business, technology, and the social sciences, and are essential for success in both academic and professional settings. Analytical skills empower students to approach problems methodically, think critically, and communicate their insights effectively.

Ideas for Study Material/Resources:
Books: "Thinking, Fast and Slow" by Daniel Kahneman, "How to Lie with Statistics" by Darrell Huff, "Data Science for Business" by Foster Provost and Tom Fawcett.
Online Courses: Platforms like Coursera, edX, and Khan Academy offer courses on analytical skills, data analysis, and critical thinking.
Articles and Blogs: Harvard Business Review, Forbes, and DataCamp often feature articles on analytical techniques and case studies.

Ideas for Activity:
Conduct data analysis workshops where participants analyze datasets, draw insights, and present their findings to the group.
Facilitate problem-solving exercises or case studies that require participants to apply analytical skills to real-world scenarios.

Some Training Ideas for Facilitation:
Start by defining analytical skills and their importance in various personal and professional contexts.
Teach techniques for gathering and analyzing data, such as data visualization, statistical analysis, and hypothesis testing.
Provide guidance on interpreting results, drawing conclusions, and making data-driven recommendations.

Did You Know?
Research shows that individuals with strong analytical skills are more likely to succeed in their careers and contribute to organizational growth and innovation.

Ideas for Presentation:
Create a PowerPoint presentation or e-book summarizing key analytical concepts, methods, and tools. Include examples of data analysis techniques and case studies to illustrate their applications.

Training Video Guide:
Develop video tutorials demonstrating various analytical techniques, such as Excel functions, data visualization tools, and statistical analysis methods. Use real-life datasets to demonstrate the process of analyzing data and drawing insights.

Skill 17: Interpersonal Skills

Importance:
Interpersonal skills, also known as people skills or social skills, are essential for building positive relationships, collaborating effectively, and resolving conflicts. They encompass communication, empathy, and the ability to relate well to others.

Concept:
Interpersonal skills involve the ability to interact with others in a respectful, empathetic, and constructive manner. They include active listening, empathy, assertiveness, and conflict resolution skills.

Takeaway: Guide for Students and Professionals
By mastering interpersonal skills, individuals can enhance their relationships, build trust, and foster a positive work environment. Strong interpersonal skills are valuable in both personal and professional contexts, enabling individuals to connect with others and navigate social interactions with ease.

For a beginner student today, mastering interpersonal skills is essential for building and maintaining positive relationships in both academic and personal settings. Interpersonal skills encompass the ability to communicate effectively, collaborate with others, and navigate social interactions with empathy and understanding.

Key components of interpersonal skills include effective communication, which involves expressing oneself clearly and listening actively to others. This means paying attention to both verbal and nonverbal cues, such as body language, tone of voice, and facial expressions, to ensure messages are understood accurately.

Empathy is another crucial aspect, as it allows students to understand and share the feelings of others, fostering trust and rapport. By showing empathy, students can create a supportive environment where peers feel valued and respected.

Collaboration is vital for working effectively in teams. This involves being open to others' ideas, contributing to group efforts, and resolving conflicts constructively. Good collaborators can balance assertiveness with cooperation, ensuring that their own views are heard while also valuing the input of others.

Problem-solving within interpersonal contexts is also important. This includes addressing misunderstandings or disagreements calmly and diplomatically, finding mutually acceptable solutions, and maintaining positive relationships even in challenging situations.

Additionally, social skills such as making introductions, engaging in small talk, and showing appreciation can enhance one's ability to connect with others. Being polite, respectful, and considerate goes a long way in building strong interpersonal relationships.

By developing strong interpersonal skills, students can enhance their ability to work collaboratively, build strong networks, and create a positive and inclusive environment. These skills are invaluable not only in academic settings but also in future professional and personal endeavors, as they enable individuals to navigate social interactions with confidence and ease.

Ideas for Study Material/Resources:
Books: "How to Win Friends and Influence People" by Dale Carnegie, "Crucial Conversations" by Kerry Patterson, Joseph Grenny, Ron McMillan, and Al Switzler, "The 5 Love Languages" by Gary Chapman.
Online Courses: Platforms like LinkedIn Learning, Coursera, and Udemy offer courses on interpersonal skills, communication, and conflict resolution.

Articles and Blogs: Psychology Today, Forbes, and MindTools often feature articles on interpersonal communication and relationship-building techniques.

Ideas for Activity:
Conduct role-playing exercises where participants practice active listening, empathetic communication, and conflict resolution in various scenarios.
Facilitate group discussions on effective communication techniques, building rapport, and managing interpersonal conflicts.

Some Training Ideas for Facilitation:
Start by defining interpersonal skills and their importance in personal and professional relationships.
Teach techniques for effective communication, including active listening, assertiveness, and non-verbal communication.
Provide guidance on building empathy, understanding different perspectives, and resolving conflicts constructively.

Did You Know?
Research shows that individuals with strong interpersonal skills are more likely to succeed in their careers, build supportive networks, and experience greater job satisfaction.

Ideas for Presentation:
Create a PowerPoint presentation or e-book summarizing key interpersonal skills concepts, communication strategies, and conflict resolution techniques. Include case studies and scenarios to illustrate effective interpersonal interactions.

Training Video Guide:
Develop video tutorials demonstrating various interpersonal skills in action, such as active listening, assertive communication, and empathy. Use role-plays and real-life examples to illustrate effective interpersonal communication.

Skill 18: Self-Awareness

Importance:
Self-awareness is the foundation of personal growth, emotional intelligence, and effective leadership. It involves understanding one's strengths, weaknesses, values, and emotions.

Concept:
Self-awareness encompasses introspection, self-reflection, and mindfulness. It involves recognizing one's thoughts, feelings, and behaviors and understanding how they impact oneself and others.

Takeaway: Guide for Students and Professionals
By mastering self-awareness, individuals can improve their decision-making, build stronger relationships, and lead with authenticity. Self-awareness fosters personal growth, resilience, and a deeper understanding of oneself and others.
For a beginner student today, cultivating self-awareness is essential for personal growth, academic success, and building healthy relationships. Self-awareness involves the ability to recognize and understand one's own emotions, thoughts, and behaviors, as well as their impact on others.

Key components of self-awareness include emotional awareness, which involves identifying and understanding one's own emotions and how they influence actions and decisions. This can help students manage their reactions and develop emotional intelligence.

Another aspect is self-reflection, which involves regularly evaluating one's strengths, weaknesses, values, and goals. By understanding what motivates them and where they need to improve, students can make more informed choices about their academic and personal lives.

Mindfulness is also an important part of self-awareness. This involves being present in the moment and paying attention to one's thoughts, feelings, and surroundings without judgment. Practicing mindfulness can reduce stress and improve focus and concentration.

Understanding one's learning style is another crucial element. Knowing whether they are visual, auditory, or kinesthetic learners, for instance, can help students tailor their study habits to be more effective and efficient.

Self-awareness also includes recognizing how one's behavior affects others. This can enhance interpersonal relationships and foster a more empathetic and respectful interaction with peers and teachers.

By developing self-awareness, students can better understand their motivations, improve their emotional regulation, set realistic goals, and build stronger relationships. This not only contributes to academic success but also to overall well-being and personal fulfillment. Self-awareness is a foundational skill that supports lifelong learning and personal development, helping students navigate the complexities of life with confidence and insight.

Ideas for Study Material/Resources:
Books: "Emotional Intelligence 2.0" by Travis Bradberry and Jean Greaves, "The Gifts of Imperfection" by Brené Brown, "Mindset: The New Psychology of Success" by Carol S. Dweck.
Online Courses: Platforms like Coursera, Insight Timer, and Mindful.org offer courses on mindfulness, self-awareness, and personal development.
Articles and Blogs: Harvard Business Review, Psychology Today, and Greater Good Magazine often feature articles on self-awareness and introspection.

Ideas for Activity:
Conduct mindfulness meditation sessions or self-awareness exercises where participants explore their thoughts, emotions, and physical sensations.
Facilitate journaling or self-assessment activities to help participants identify their strengths, values, and areas for growth.

Some Training Ideas for Facilitation:
Start by defining self-awareness and its importance in personal and professional development.
Teach techniques for developing self-awareness, such as mindfulness practices, journaling, and seeking feedback from others.
Provide guidance on cultivating a growth mindset, embracing vulnerability, and fostering self-compassion.

Did You Know?
Research shows that individuals who are self-aware are more likely to achieve their goals, experience greater job satisfaction, and build fulfilling relationships.

Ideas for Presentation:
Create a PowerPoint presentation or e-book summarizing key self-awareness concepts, mindfulness exercises, and reflection prompts. Include examples and case studies to illustrate the benefits of self-awareness.

Training Video Guide:
Develop video tutorials demonstrating various self-awareness practices, such as mindfulness meditation, self-reflection exercises, and feedback-seeking techniques. Use real-life examples to illustrate the impact of self-awareness on personal growth and well-being.

Skill 19: Conflict Resolution/Management

Importance:
Conflict resolution/management skills are essential for navigating disagreements, fostering collaboration, and maintaining positive relationships. They involve communication, empathy, and problem-solving techniques to address conflicts constructively.

Concept:
Conflict resolution/management encompasses the ability to identify, address, and resolve conflicts in a constructive manner. It involves active listening, understanding different perspectives, and finding mutually beneficial solutions.

Takeaway: Guide for Students and Professionals
By mastering conflict resolution/management skills, individuals can minimize tensions, promote teamwork, and create a more harmonious environment. Effective conflict resolution fosters trust, respect, and collaboration among team members.

For a beginner student today, mastering conflict resolution and management is essential for maintaining healthy relationships and creating a positive learning environment. Conflict resolution involves the ability to address and resolve disputes or disagreements constructively and respectfully.

Key components of conflict resolution include active listening, which involves fully concentrating on what the other person is saying without interrupting, ensuring that each party feels heard and understood. This helps to clarify the issues at hand and fosters mutual respect.

Effective communication is also crucial. This means expressing one's own perspective and feelings clearly and assertively, without being aggressive or dismissive. Using "I" statements, such as "I feel" or "I think," can help to convey one's message without blaming or criticizing others.

Empathy plays a vital role in conflict resolution. Understanding and acknowledging the other person's feelings and viewpoints can defuse tension and create an atmosphere of cooperation. It shows that you respect and value the other person's perspective, even if you do not agree with it.

Problem-solving skills are essential for finding mutually acceptable solutions. This involves brainstorming possible solutions, evaluating the pros and cons of each option, and agreeing on a course of action that satisfies all parties involved. Being open to compromise and willing to find a middle ground is key.

Additionally, maintaining emotional control is important during conflicts. Staying calm and composed, even when emotions are running high, helps prevent the situation from escalating and allows for more rational and productive discussions.

Setting boundaries and knowing when to involve a mediator or seek help from a third party, such as a teacher or counselor, can also be crucial in managing conflicts that cannot be resolved independently.

By developing strong conflict resolution and management skills, students can enhance their ability to handle disagreements constructively, build stronger relationships, and create a more harmonious and collaborative environment. These skills are valuable not only in academic settings but also in personal and professional life, contributing to overall success and well-being.

Ideas for Study Material/Resources:
Books: "Getting to Yes: Negotiating Agreement Without Giving In" by Roger Fisher, William Ury, and Bruce Patton, "Crucial Conversations" by Kerry Patterson, Joseph Grenny, Ron McMillan, and Al Switzler, "Difficult Conversations: How to Discuss What Matters Most" by Douglas Stone, Bruce Patton, and Sheila Heen.
Online Courses: Platforms like Coursera, LinkedIn Learning, and Udemy offer courses on conflict resolution, negotiation, and communication skills.

Articles and Blogs: Harvard Business Review, Psychology Today, and Mediate.com often feature articles on conflict resolution techniques and case studies.

Ideas for Activity:
Conduct role-playing exercises where participants practice resolving conflicts in various scenarios, such as workplace disagreements or interpersonal conflicts.
Facilitate group discussions on conflict resolution strategies, communication techniques, and de-escalation tactics.

Some Training Ideas for Facilitation:
Start by defining conflict resolution/management and its importance in fostering positive relationships and teamwork.
Teach techniques for managing emotions, active listening, and reframing perspectives during conflicts.
Provide guidance on facilitating constructive conversations, finding common ground, and negotiating mutually acceptable solutions.

Did You Know?
Research shows that teams that effectively resolve conflicts are more cohesive, productive, and innovative than those that avoid or escalate conflicts.

Ideas for Presentation:
Create a PowerPoint presentation or e-book summarizing key conflict resolution/management concepts, communication strategies, and negotiation techniques. Include case studies and examples to illustrate effective conflict resolution in action.

Training Video Guide:
Develop video tutorials demonstrating various conflict resolution techniques, such as active listening, reframing, and mediation. Use role-plays and real-life scenarios to illustrate effective conflict resolution strategies.

Skill 20: Networking Skills

Importance:
Networking skills are essential for building professional relationships, expanding one's social and professional circle, and advancing one's career. They involve communication, relationship-building, and social etiquette.

Concept:
Networking skills encompass the ability to connect with others, cultivate relationships, and leverage opportunities for mutual benefit. They involve effective communication, active listening, and strategic relationship-building.

Takeaway: Guide for Students and Professionals
By mastering networking skills, individuals can expand their professional network, access new opportunities, and stay informed about industry trends. Effective networking fosters collaboration, mentorship, and career advancement.

For a beginner student today, mastering conflict resolution and management is essential for maintaining healthy relationships and creating a positive learning environment. Conflict resolution involves the ability to address and resolve disputes or disagreements constructively and respectfully.

Key components of conflict resolution include active listening, which involves fully concentrating on what the other person is saying without interrupting, ensuring that each party feels heard and understood. This helps to clarify the issues at hand and fosters mutual respect.

Effective communication is also crucial. This means expressing one's own perspective and feelings clearly and assertively, without being aggressive or dismissive. Using "I" statements, such as "I feel" or "I think," can help to convey one's message without blaming or criticizing others.

Empathy plays a vital role in conflict resolution. Understanding and acknowledging the other person's feelings and viewpoints can defuse tension and create an atmosphere of cooperation. It shows that you respect and value the other person's perspective, even if you do not agree with it.

Problem-solving skills are essential for finding mutually acceptable solutions. This involves brainstorming possible solutions, evaluating the pros and cons of each option, and agreeing on a course of action that satisfies all parties involved. Being open to compromise and willing to find a middle ground is key.

Additionally, maintaining emotional control is important during conflicts. Staying calm and composed, even when emotions are running high, helps prevent the situation from escalating and allows for more rational and productive discussions.

Setting boundaries and knowing when to involve a mediator or seek help from a third party, such as a teacher or counselor, can also be crucial in managing conflicts that cannot be resolved independently.

By developing strong conflict resolution and management skills, students can enhance their ability to handle disagreements constructively, build stronger relationships, and create a more harmonious and collaborative environment. These skills are valuable not only in academic settings but also in personal and professional life, contributing to overall success and well-being.

Ideas for Study Material/Resources:
Books: "Never Eat Alone" by Keith Ferrazzi, "How to Talk to Anyone" by Leil Lowndes, "The Startup of You" by Reid Hoffman and Ben Casnocha.

Online Courses: Platforms like LinkedIn Learning, Coursera, and Udemy offer courses on networking skills, relationship-building, and personal branding.
Articles and Blogs: Forbes, Entrepreneur, and Inc. often feature articles on networking strategies, professional etiquette, and relationship-building techniques.

Ideas for Activity:
Conduct networking events or mixers where participants have the opportunity to meet and connect with others in their industry or field.
Facilitate networking exercises such as elevator pitches, informational interviews, or group discussions on professional topics.

Some Training Ideas for Facilitation:
Start by defining networking skills and their importance in career development and professional success.
Teach techniques for effective networking, such as researching contacts, initiating conversations, and following up with connections.
Provide guidance on building and maintaining professional relationships, cultivating a personal brand, and leveraging social media for networking.

Did You Know?
Research shows that a significant percentage of job opportunities and business deals are found through networking and referrals rather than traditional job postings or advertising.

Ideas for Presentation:
Create a PowerPoint presentation or e-book summarizing key networking concepts, strategies for building professional relationships, and tips for effective networking. Include case studies and success stories to illustrate the power of networking.

Training Video Guide:
Develop video tutorials demonstrating various networking techniques, such as networking events, informational interviews, and online networking platforms. Use real-life examples to illustrate effective networking strategies and best practices.

Skill 21: Digital Skills/Literacy

Importance:
Digital skills/literacy are essential in today's technology-driven world, enabling individuals to navigate digital tools, platforms, and information effectively. They encompass proficiency in using computers, the internet, and digital devices for communication, research, and productivity.

Concept:
Digital skills/literacy involve the ability to use digital technologies confidently and competently. They include basic computer skills, internet literacy, data literacy, and cybersecurity awareness.

Takeaway: Guide for Students and Professionals
By mastering digital skills/literacy, individuals can enhance their employability, productivity, and access to information. Digital literacy empowers individuals to communicate, collaborate, and innovate in a digital environment.

For a beginner student today, mastering digital skills and literacy is essential for navigating the increasingly digital world in which we live, study, and work. Digital literacy involves the ability to use technology effectively and responsibly to communicate, access information, solve problems, and create content.

Key components of digital skills and literacy include:

1. Basic Computer Skills : Understanding how to operate computers and other digital devices, including tasks such as using word processors, spreadsheets, and presentation software. Familiarity with operating systems, file management, and basic troubleshooting is also important.

2. Internet Navigation : Knowing how to efficiently search for information online using search engines, evaluate the credibility of websites, and understand internet safety practices to protect personal information and avoid scams.

3. Communication Tools : Proficiency with email, instant messaging, video conferencing, and social media platforms. This includes understanding the appropriate use of different communication tools and maintaining professional and respectful digital communication.

4. Digital Content Creation : The ability to create and edit digital content, such as documents, presentations, videos, and graphics. This includes using various software and tools to produce high-quality work and understanding copyright and intellectual property rights.

5. Online Collaboration : Familiarity with tools that facilitate online collaboration, such as cloud storage services, collaborative document editing, and project management platforms. This includes understanding how to share files, work on group projects, and manage digital workflows.

6. Digital Citizenship : Understanding the ethical and responsible use of technology, including respecting others' privacy, avoiding cyberbullying, and adhering to online etiquette. It also involves understanding the impact of one's digital footprint and practicing safe online behavior.

7. Problem-Solving with Technology : The ability to leverage digital tools and resources to solve problems and improve efficiency. This includes using software for data analysis, project planning, and research.

8. Learning Management Systems (LMS) : Familiarity with platforms used in educational settings to access course materials, submit assignments, participate in discussions, and track academic progress.

By developing strong digital skills and literacy, students can enhance their ability to learn, communicate, and collaborate effectively in an increasingly digital world. These skills are essential for academic success, future career opportunities, and everyday life, enabling students to navigate digital environments with confidence and competence.

Ideas for Study Material/Resources:
Books: "Digital Literacy for Dummies" by Faithe Wempen, "The Google Infused Classroom" by Holly Clark and Tanya Avrith, "The Art of SEO" by Eric Enge, Stephan Spencer, and Jessie Stricchiola.
Online Courses: Platforms like LinkedIn Learning, Coursera, and Google Digital Garage offer courses on digital skills, internet safety, and data literacy.
Articles and Blogs: TechCrunch, Wired, and Mashable often feature articles on digital literacy, cybersecurity, and emerging technologies.

Ideas for Activity:
Conduct workshops or training sessions on basic computer skills, internet safety, and data literacy.
Facilitate hands-on activities where participants practice using digital tools and platforms for various tasks, such as email communication, online research, and document creation.

Some Training Ideas for Facilitation:
Start by defining digital skills/literacy and their importance in today's digital age.
Teach basic computer skills, such as using operating systems, word processing software, and web browsers.
Provide guidance on internet safety, data privacy, and best practices for online communication and collaboration.

Did You Know?
Research shows that individuals with strong digital skills are more likely to succeed in the workplace and adapt to technological changes effectively.

Ideas for Presentation:
Create a PowerPoint presentation or e-book summarizing key digital skills/literacy concepts, online safety tips, and resources for further learning. Include interactive elements and video tutorials to enhance engagement.

Training Video Guide:
Develop video tutorials demonstrating various digital skills, such as navigating software applications, conducting online research, and protecting against cyber threats. Use step-by-step demonstrations and real-life examples to illustrate key concepts.

Skill 22: Data Analysis

Importance:
Data analysis skills are essential for interpreting and making sense of data to inform decision-making, solve problems, and drive business outcomes. They encompass statistical analysis, data visualization, and interpretation of findings.

Concept:
Data analysis involves the process of examining data sets to extract insights, identify trends, and draw conclusions. It includes techniques such as descriptive statistics, inferential statistics, regression analysis, and data visualization.

Takeaway: Guide for Students and Professionals
By mastering data analysis skills, individuals can make data-driven decisions, identify opportunities for improvement, and communicate insights effectively. Data analysis enables organizations to optimize processes, innovate, and stay competitive in a data-driven world. For a beginner student today, mastering data analysis is crucial for understanding and interpreting the vast amounts of information encountered in both academic and professional settings. Data analysis involves collecting, processing, and examining data to extract meaningful insights and support informed decision-making.

Key components of data analysis include:

1. Understanding Data Types : Recognizing different types of data (quantitative vs. qualitative, discrete vs. continuous) and knowing how to handle each type appropriately.

2. Data Collection : Learning methods for gathering accurate and relevant data from various sources, such as surveys, experiments, databases, and online resources.

3. Data Cleaning : Ensuring the data is accurate and free from errors by identifying and correcting inconsistencies, missing values, and outliers. This step is crucial for maintaining data integrity.

4. Statistical Techniques : Familiarity with basic statistical concepts and techniques, such as mean, median, mode, standard deviation, correlation, and regression analysis. These tools help summarize and describe data patterns.

5. Software Proficiency : Gaining proficiency in data analysis software and tools such as Microsoft Excel, Google Sheets, R, Python, SPSS, or other specialized programs. These tools facilitate data manipulation, visualization, and complex analyses.

6. Data Visualization : The ability to present data findings in a clear and visually appealing manner using charts, graphs, and dashboards. Effective data visualization helps communicate insights more effectively to a broader audience.

7. Interpretation of Results : Developing the skill to draw meaningful conclusions from data analysis, understanding the implications of the results, and being able to explain the significance in a clear and concise manner.

8. Critical Thinking : Applying critical thinking to question assumptions, identify potential biases, and evaluate the reliability and validity of the data and the analysis.

9. Ethical Considerations : Understanding the ethical implications of data collection, analysis, and reporting. This includes respecting privacy, ensuring confidentiality, and avoiding misrepresentation of data.

By developing strong data analysis skills, students can enhance their ability to make data-driven decisions, support their arguments with evidence, and contribute valuable insights in both academic research and real-world applications. These skills are highly valued in many fields, including science, business, healthcare, and technology, and are essential for success in the modern, data-rich world.

Ideas for Study Material/Resources:
Books: "Data Science for Business" by Foster Provost and Tom Fawcett, "Naked Statistics: Stripping the Dread from the Data" by Charles Wheelan, "Storytelling with Data" by Cole Nussbaumer Knaflic.
Online Courses: Platforms like Coursera, edX, and DataCamp offer courses on data analysis, statistics, and data visualization.
Articles and Blogs: Towards Data Science, Dataquest, and KDnuggets often feature articles on data analysis techniques, case studies, and industry trends.

Ideas for Activity:
Conduct data analysis workshops where participants analyze real-life datasets, perform statistical tests, and interpret findings.
Facilitate group discussions on best practices for data analysis, data visualization techniques, and storytelling with data.

Some Training Ideas for Facilitation:
Start by defining data analysis and its importance in decision-making and problem-solving.
Teach techniques for data cleaning, exploratory data analysis, hypothesis testing, and interpreting results.
Provide guidance on using data visualization tools, storytelling techniques, and presenting insights effectively.

Did You Know?
Research shows that organizations that leverage data analysis effectively are more likely to outperform their competitors and achieve strategic goals.

Ideas for Presentation:
Create a PowerPoint presentation or e-book summarizing key data analysis concepts, statistical techniques, and data visualization best practices. Include case studies and examples to illustrate the application of data analysis in different domains.

Training Video Guide:
Develop video tutorials demonstrating various data analysis techniques, such as data cleaning, hypothesis testing, and creating data visualizations. Use real-life datasets and examples to illustrate the process of analyzing data and deriving insights.

Skill 23: Project Management

Importance:
Project management skills are crucial for planning, executing, and monitoring projects to ensure they are completed on time, within budget, and according to specifications. They involve leadership, organization, and communication to coordinate resources and achieve project goals.

Concept:
Project management encompasses the processes, methodologies, and tools used to initiate, plan, execute, monitor, and close projects. It includes defining project scope, setting objectives, allocating resources, and managing risks.

Takeaway: Guide for Students and Professionals
By mastering project management skills, individuals can lead projects effectively, meet deadlines, and deliver results. Project management enables organizations to achieve strategic objectives, maximize efficiency, and adapt to change.

For a beginner student today, mastering project management is essential for successfully planning, executing, and completing projects in both academic and personal contexts. Project management involves coordinating tasks, managing resources, and ensuring that goals are achieved within specified constraints such as time, budget, and scope.

Key components of project management include:

1.   Planning : Developing a detailed project plan that outlines the objectives, deliverables, timelines, and resources needed. This includes defining the project scope and setting clear, achievable goals.

2. Task Management : Breaking down the project into smaller, manageable tasks. Creating a task list or a work breakdown structure (WBS) helps to organize and prioritize these tasks.

3. Scheduling : Using tools like Gantt charts or project management software to create a project schedule. This helps track progress, manage deadlines, and ensure timely completion of tasks.

4. Resource Allocation : Identifying and allocating the necessary resources, such as people, materials, and budget, to ensure that each task can be completed efficiently.

5. Risk Management : Anticipating potential risks and challenges that may arise during the project. Developing contingency plans to mitigate these risks ensures that the project can proceed smoothly despite obstacles.

6. Communication : Establishing clear communication channels among all stakeholders. Regular updates, meetings, and reports keep everyone informed and engaged, facilitating collaboration and problem-solving.

7. Team Management : Leading and motivating the project team. This involves assigning roles and responsibilities, providing guidance, and fostering a positive and productive team environment.

8. Monitoring and Control : Continuously monitoring the project's progress against the plan. Using key performance indicators (KPIs) and milestones to measure success and make necessary adjustments to stay on track.

9. Quality Management : Ensuring that the project's deliverables meet the required standards and specifications. This involves setting quality criteria and conducting regular reviews and tests.

10. Documentation and Reporting : Maintaining accurate records of the project's progress, decisions, and changes. Providing regular status reports to stakeholders keeps them informed and helps manage expectations.

11. Closure : Completing all project tasks, delivering the final product, and obtaining stakeholder approval. Conducting a post-project review to evaluate what went well and what could be improved for future projects.

By developing strong project management skills, students can enhance their ability to organize and execute projects effectively, leading to successful outcomes and the achievement of their goals. These skills are valuable not only in academic settings but also in professional environments, where effective project management is critical to success. Project management skills empower students to take control of complex tasks, work collaboratively, and deliver high-quality results.

Ideas for Study Material/Resources:
Books: "The Project Management Book" by Richard Newton, "Scrum: The Art of Doing Twice the Work in Half the Time" by Jeff Sutherland, "Getting Things Done" by David Allen.
Online Courses: Platforms like Coursera, Project Management Institute (PMI), and Udemy offer courses on project management methodologies, tools, and best practices.
Articles and Blogs: ProjectManagement.com, PMI.org, and Harvard Business Review often feature articles on project management techniques, case studies, and industry trends.

Ideas for Activity:
Conduct project management workshops where participants work on simulated projects, create project plans, and allocate resources.
Facilitate group discussions on project management methodologies, such as Agile, Waterfall, and Scrum, and their applications in different contexts.

Some Training Ideas for Facilitation:
Start by defining project management and its importance in achieving project success. Teach project management methodologies, tools, and techniques for planning, scheduling, budgeting, and risk management.
Provide guidance on leadership skills, team management, stakeholder communication, and conflict resolution in project environments.

Did You Know?
Research shows that organizations with effective project management practices are more likely to deliver projects on time and within budget, leading to higher customer satisfaction and ROI.

Ideas for Presentation:
Create a PowerPoint presentation or e-book summarizing key project management concepts, methodologies, and best practices. Include templates, checklists, and case studies to illustrate project management principles.

Training Video Guide:
Develop video tutorials demonstrating various project management techniques, such as creating project plans, managing stakeholders, and conducting project meetings. Use real-life examples and case studies to illustrate effective project management in action.

Skill 24: Financial Literacy

Importance:
Financial literacy skills are essential for understanding personal and business finances, making informed financial decisions, and achieving financial goals. They involve knowledge of financial concepts, budgeting, investing, and debt management.

Concept:
Financial literacy encompasses the ability to understand financial statements, manage budgets, evaluate investment options, and plan for long-term financial security. It includes concepts such as budgeting, saving, investing, and managing debt.

Takeaway: Guide for Students and Professionals
By mastering financial literacy skills, individuals can take control of their finances, build wealth, and achieve financial independence. Financial literacy enables individuals to make informed decisions about saving, spending, and investing their money.

For a beginner student today, mastering financial literacy is essential for making informed decisions about managing money and planning for the future. Financial literacy involves understanding and effectively using various financial skills, including personal financial management, budgeting, saving, investing, and understanding credit.

Key components of financial literacy include:

1. Budgeting : Learning how to create and stick to a budget. This involves tracking income and expenses, distinguishing between needs and wants, and planning for regular expenses and savings. A budget helps students manage their money, avoid debt, and save for future goals.

2. Saving : Understanding the importance of saving money for emergencies, large purchases, and future needs. This includes setting up a savings account, establishing savings goals, and developing the habit of regularly setting aside a portion of income.

3. Banking : Gaining knowledge about different types of bank accounts (checking, savings), how to use them, and understanding fees and interest rates. Students should also learn how to manage online banking tools for convenience and efficiency.

4. Credit and Debt Management : Understanding how credit works, including credit scores, credit reports, and interest rates. Knowing how to use credit responsibly, avoid excessive debt, and manage credit card use is crucial for maintaining financial health.

5. Investing : Learning the basics of investing, including different types of investments (stocks, bonds, mutual funds), the principles of risk and return, and the importance of starting to invest early to benefit from compound interest. Understanding investment strategies can help students grow their wealth over time.

6. Taxes : Familiarizing oneself with the basics of taxation, including how to read a pay stub, understanding deductions, and learning how to file a tax return. Knowing about taxes helps students prepare for tax obligations and maximize potential refunds.

7. Financial Planning : Setting short-term and long-term financial goals, such as buying a car, paying for education, or saving for retirement. Financial planning involves creating a roadmap for achieving these goals through careful management of income, expenses, savings, and investments.

8. Insurance : Understanding the different types of insurance (health, auto, renters, life) and their importance in protecting against financial loss. Knowing how to choose the right insurance coverage can provide financial security.

9. Consumer Awareness : Developing the ability to make informed purchasing decisions, recognize predatory lending practices, and understand consumer rights. This includes knowing how to compare products, read contracts, and avoid scams.

10. Financial Tools and Resources : Utilizing financial tools and resources, such as budgeting apps, financial calculators, and educational websites, to enhance financial knowledge and skills.

By developing strong financial literacy skills, students can take control of their financial futures, make informed decisions, and achieve financial stability and independence. These skills are valuable not only for managing personal finances but also for understanding broader economic concepts and participating effectively in the financial aspects of adult life. Financial literacy empowers students to make wise financial choices and build a solid foundation for their future.

Ideas for Study Material/Resources:
Books: "Rich Dad Poor Dad" by Robert T. Kiyosaki, "The Total Money Makeover" by Dave Ramsey, "I Will Teach You to Be Rich" by Ramit Sethi.
Online Courses: Platforms like Coursera, Khan Academy, and Investopedia offer courses on personal finance, investing, and financial planning.
Articles and Blogs: The Financial Diet, NerdWallet, and The Motley Fool often feature articles on personal finance tips, investment strategies, and financial planning advice.

Ideas for Activity:
Conduct financial literacy workshops where participants learn about budgeting, saving, investing, and debt management through interactive exercises and case studies.
Facilitate group discussions on financial goals, risk tolerance, and strategies for achieving financial independence.

Some Training Ideas for Facilitation:
Start by defining financial literacy and its importance in achieving financial well-being. Teach basic financial concepts such as budgeting, saving, investing, and managing debt.
Provide guidance on creating financial plans, setting financial goals, and developing strategies for building wealth over time.

Did You Know?
Research shows that individuals with higher levels of financial literacy are more likely to make sound financial decisions, accumulate wealth, and achieve financial security.

Ideas for Presentation:
Create a PowerPoint presentation or e-book summarizing key financial literacy concepts, budgeting techniques, investment strategies, and debt management tips. Include interactive elements and real-life examples to illustrate financial principles.

Training Video Guide:
Develop video tutorials demonstrating various financial literacy topics, such as creating a budget, investing in stocks, and managing credit. Use visual aids and real-life scenarios to explain complex financial concepts in an accessible way.

Skill 25: Research Skills

Importance:
Research skills are essential for gathering, analyzing, and interpreting information to solve problems, make decisions, and advance knowledge. They involve critical thinking, information literacy, and attention to detail.

Concept:
Research skills encompass the ability to identify research questions, conduct literature reviews, gather data, and draw conclusions based on evidence. They include skills such as data analysis, citation management, and research ethics.

Takeaway: Guide for Students and Professionals
By mastering research skills, individuals can conduct high-quality research, contribute to knowledge creation, and make informed decisions based on evidence. Research skills are valuable in academic, professional, and personal contexts.

For a beginner student today, mastering research skills is essential for academic success and lifelong learning. Research skills involve the ability to locate, evaluate, and use information effectively to answer questions, solve problems, and support arguments.

Key components of research skills include:

1. Defining a Research Question : Starting with a clear, focused research question or hypothesis. This involves identifying a topic of interest, narrowing it down to a specific question, and determining the scope of the research.

2. Information Literacy : Understanding how to locate and access relevant information using various sources, including libraries, academic databases, and the internet. This involves knowing how to use search engines, keywords, and Boolean operators to find the most pertinent information.

3. Evaluating Sources : Assessing the credibility, reliability, and relevance of information sources. This includes distinguishing between primary and secondary sources, recognizing biased or unreliable information, and evaluating the authority and expertise of authors.

4. Note-Taking and Organization : Developing effective note-taking strategies to record important information, ideas, and references. Organizing notes systematically, whether digitally or on paper, helps in synthesizing information and writing reports or papers.

5. Critical Thinking : Analyzing and interpreting information critically. This involves identifying key points, understanding different perspectives, and evaluating the evidence supporting various claims.

6. Citation and Referencing : Understanding the importance of citing sources correctly to avoid plagiarism and give proper credit to original authors. Familiarity with different citation styles (e.g., APA, MLA, Chicago) and using tools like citation managers can help ensure accuracy.

7. Data Collection and Analysis : For empirical research, knowing how to design and conduct experiments, surveys, or observations. This includes collecting data systematically, analyzing it using appropriate methods, and interpreting the results.

8. Synthesis and Integration : Combining information from various sources to build a coherent understanding of the topic. This involves comparing and contrasting different viewpoints, identifying trends, and synthesizing findings into a comprehensive analysis.

9. Writing and Presentation : Communicating research findings effectively through well-organized reports, essays, or presentations. This includes structuring the content logically, using clear and concise language, and supporting arguments with evidence.

10. Ethical Considerations : Understanding and adhering to ethical standards in research, such as obtaining consent for studies involving human subjects, ensuring confidentiality, and presenting findings honestly and transparently.

By developing strong research skills, students can enhance their ability to gather and analyze information, think critically, and communicate their findings effectively. These skills are essential for academic success, enabling students to produce high-quality work and contribute meaningfully to their fields of study. Additionally, research skills are valuable in professional and personal contexts, fostering a lifelong ability to learn, adapt, and solve problems.

Ideas for Study Material/Resources:
Books: "The Craft of Research" by Wayne C. Booth, Gregory G. Colomb, and Joseph M. Williams, "Research Design" by John W. Creswell, "The Literature Review: A Step-by-Step Guide for Students" by Diana Ridley.
Online Courses: Platforms like Coursera, edX, and LinkedIn Learning offer courses on research methods, data analysis, and academic writing.
Articles and Blogs: Academic journals, research websites, and blogs in specific fields often publish articles on research methodologies, best practices, and case studies.

Ideas for Activity:
Conduct research methodology workshops where participants learn about different research methods, data collection techniques, and analysis tools.
Assign research projects or case studies where participants apply research skills to investigate specific topics and present their findings.

Some Training Ideas for Facilitation:
Start by defining research skills and their importance in generating knowledge and solving problems.

Teach research methodologies, including qualitative and quantitative approaches, experimental design, and survey methods.
Provide guidance on literature review techniques, data analysis tools, and ethical considerations in research.

Did You Know?
Research skills are not only valuable in academia but also in various industries, including market research, healthcare, education, and policy analysis.

Ideas for Presentation:
Create a PowerPoint presentation or e-book summarizing key research skills, research methodologies, and best practices. Include examples of research projects and tips for conducting effective research.

Training Video Guide:
Develop video tutorials demonstrating various research techniques, such as conducting literature reviews, designing surveys, and analyzing data. Use case studies and real-life examples to illustrate the research process from start to finish.

Skill 26: Sales Skills

Importance:
Sales skills are essential for persuading customers, closing deals, and driving revenue for businesses. They involve communication, negotiation, and relationship-building to meet sales targets and exceed customer expectations.

Concept:
Sales skills encompass the ability to identify customer needs, present product or service solutions, overcome objections, and negotiate terms. They include skills such as active listening, rapport-building, and objection handling.

Takeaway: Guide for Students and Professionals
By mastering sales skills, individuals can succeed in sales roles, build long-term customer relationships, and drive business growth. Sales skills are valuable in various industries, including retail, real estate, technology, and finance.

For a beginner student today, mastering sales skills is valuable for developing interpersonal communication abilities, persuasion techniques, and understanding customer needs. Sales skills are essential not only for careers directly related to sales but also for various roles in business, marketing, and entrepreneurship.

Key components of sales skills include:

1. Communication : Developing strong verbal and non-verbal communication skills to effectively convey information and build rapport with customers. This includes active listening, asking relevant questions, and tailoring communication to the needs and preferences of the audience.

2. Product Knowledge : Understanding the features, benefits, and unique selling points of the product or service being offered. Having comprehensive product knowledge allows salespeople to address customer inquiries, overcome objections, and highlight the value proposition effectively.

3. Customer Relationship Management (CRM) : Building and maintaining positive relationships with customers through personalized interactions, follow-ups, and customer service. Building trust and loyalty with customers can lead to repeat business and referrals.

4. Understanding Customer Needs : Identifying and understanding the specific needs, preferences, and pain points of potential customers. This involves asking probing questions, empathizing with their concerns, and offering solutions that meet their requirements.

5. Problem-Solving : Being able to address customer objections and concerns effectively by offering solutions and overcoming obstacles. This requires creativity, resourcefulness, and a focus on finding win-win solutions.

6. Closing Skills : Knowing how to ask for the sale and guide the customer towards making a purchasing decision. This involves recognizing buying signals, handling objections confidently, and closing the deal in a persuasive manner.

7. Negotiation Skills : Being able to negotiate terms, prices, and agreements with customers or clients to reach mutually beneficial outcomes. This includes understanding negotiation tactics, maintaining flexibility, and striving for a fair compromise.

8. Time Management : Managing time effectively to prioritize tasks, follow up with leads, and meet sales targets. This involves setting goals, planning activities, and staying organized to maximize productivity.

9. Resilience and Persistence : Developing resilience to handle rejection and setbacks, as well as maintaining a positive attitude and motivation to persist in the face of challenges. Successful salespeople understand that rejection is part of the process and use it as an opportunity to learn and improve.

10. Continuous Learning : Being open to learning and adapting to changes in the market, customer preferences, and industry trends. Continuous learning helps sales professionals stay competitive and innovative in their approach.

By developing strong sales skills, students can enhance their ability to influence others, build relationships, and achieve desired outcomes in various personal and professional contexts. These skills are valuable not only for careers in sales but also for entrepreneurship, leadership, and customer service roles, as they contribute to overall success and effectiveness in working with others.

Ideas for Study Material/Resources:
Books: "SPIN Selling" by Neil Rackham, "Influence: The Psychology of Persuasion" by Robert B. Cialdini, "The Challenger Sale" by Matthew Dixon and Brent Adamson.
Online Courses: Platforms like Udemy, Skillshare, and Sales Hacker offer courses on sales techniques, negotiation skills, and customer relationship management.
Articles and Blogs: Sales publications, industry blogs, and sales training websites often feature articles on sales strategies, sales process optimization, and sales success stories.

Ideas for Activity:
Conduct sales role-playing exercises where participants practice sales scenarios, such as cold calling, objection handling, and closing deals.
Organize sales pitch competitions or mock sales presentations where participants demonstrate their sales skills and receive feedback.

Some Training Ideas for Facilitation:
Start by defining sales skills and their importance in driving revenue and building customer relationships.
Teach sales methodologies, including consultative selling, solution selling, and relationship selling.
Provide guidance on sales techniques, such as building rapport, qualifying leads, delivering persuasive presentations, and handling objections.

Did You Know?
Effective sales skills not only drive revenue but also contribute to customer satisfaction, loyalty, and referrals, leading to long-term business success.

Ideas for Presentation:
Create a PowerPoint presentation or e-book summarizing key sales skills, sales techniques, and best practices. Include case studies and examples to illustrate successful sales strategies and approaches.

Training Video Guide:
Develop video tutorials demonstrating various sales techniques, such as effective cold calling, consultative selling, and objection handling. Use role-plays and real-life scenarios to illustrate successful sales interactions and outcomes.

Skill 27: Marketing Skills

Importance:
Marketing skills are essential for promoting products, services, or ideas to target audiences and achieving business objectives. They involve strategic planning, creativity, and effective communication to attract and retain customers.

Concept:
Marketing skills encompass a wide range of activities, including market research, branding, advertising, digital marketing, and content creation. They aim to create awareness, generate interest, and drive action among potential customers.

Takeaway: Guide for Students and Professionals
By mastering marketing skills, individuals can create compelling marketing campaigns, engage with audiences across various channels, and contribute to business growth. Marketing skills are valuable in industries such as retail, hospitality, technology, and entertainment.

For a beginner student today, mastering marketing skills is essential for understanding consumer behavior, creating compelling messages, and promoting products or services effectively. Marketing skills are valuable not only for careers directly related to marketing but also for various roles in business, entrepreneurship, and communication.

Key components of marketing skills include:

1. Understanding Consumer Behavior : Gaining insights into the needs, preferences, and behaviors of target audiences. This involves conducting market research, analyzing demographic data, and identifying trends to inform marketing strategies.

2. Market Segmentation : Dividing the market into distinct groups of consumers with similar characteristics or needs. This allows marketers to tailor their messages and offerings to specific segments, maximizing relevance and effectiveness.

3. Brand Management : Building and maintaining strong brands that resonate with target audiences. This includes developing brand identity, positioning, and messaging that differentiate the brand from competitors and create emotional connections with consumers.

4. Marketing Strategy Development : Creating comprehensive marketing plans that outline goals, target markets, positioning, and tactics for reaching objectives. This involves considering factors such as product features, pricing, distribution channels, and promotional activities.

5. Content Creation and Copywriting : Developing compelling content and copy that engages audiences and communicates key messages effectively. This includes writing persuasive headlines, taglines, and advertising copy for various channels, such as websites, social media, and advertisements.

6. Digital Marketing : Understanding digital channels and tools for reaching and engaging target audiences online. This includes search engine optimization (SEO), social media marketing, email marketing, content marketing, and online advertising.

7. Marketing Analytics : Using data and analytics to measure the effectiveness of marketing campaigns, track key performance indicators (KPIs), and optimize marketing

efforts. This involves analyzing metrics such as website traffic, conversion rates, and customer engagement to inform decision-making.

8. Creative Problem-Solving : Finding innovative solutions to marketing challenges and adapting strategies to changing market conditions. This requires creativity, flexibility, and a willingness to experiment and iterate based on feedback and results.

9. Customer Relationship Management (CRM) : Building and nurturing relationships with customers through personalized interactions, customer service, and loyalty programs. This involves understanding customer needs and preferences, anticipating their questions and concerns, and providing solutions that meet their expectations.

10. Networking and Collaboration : Developing relationships with industry peers, partners, and influencers to expand reach and opportunities. This includes attending industry events, participating in professional associations, and leveraging social networks for networking and collaboration.

By developing strong marketing skills, students can enhance their ability to promote products or services effectively, engage with target audiences, and drive business growth. These skills are valuable not only for careers in marketing but also for entrepreneurship, sales, customer service, and leadership roles, as they contribute to overall success and competitiveness in the marketplace. Marketing skills empower students to understand market dynamics, influence consumer behavior, and create value for businesses and consumers alike.

Ideas for Study Material/Resources:
Books: "Influence: The Psychology of Persuasion" by Robert B. Cialdini, "Contagious: How to Build Word of Mouth in the Digital Age" by Jonah Berger, "Building a StoryBrand" by Donald Miller.
Online Courses: Platforms like Coursera, HubSpot Academy, and Google Digital Garage offer courses on marketing fundamentals, digital marketing, and social media marketing.
Articles and Blogs: Marketing publications, industry blogs, and marketing agency websites often feature articles on marketing strategies, trends, and case studies.

Ideas for Activity:
Conduct marketing strategy workshops where participants develop marketing plans, identify target audiences, and brainstorm creative campaign ideas.
Organize marketing simulation games or case studies where participants apply marketing principles to solve real-world marketing challenges.

Some Training Ideas for Facilitation:
Start by defining marketing skills and their role in creating value for customers and businesses.
Teach marketing fundamentals, including market segmentation, positioning, pricing strategies, and marketing mix elements (product, price, place, promotion).
Provide guidance on digital marketing techniques, such as search engine optimization (SEO), social media marketing, email marketing, and content marketing.

Did You Know?
Effective marketing skills not only drive sales but also build brand awareness, loyalty, and advocacy, resulting in long-term business success.

Ideas for Presentation:
Create a PowerPoint presentation or e-book summarizing key marketing skills, marketing strategies, and best practices. Include case studies and examples to illustrate successful marketing campaigns and initiatives.

Training Video Guide:
Develop video tutorials demonstrating various marketing techniques, such as creating social media content, running advertising campaigns, and analyzing marketing metrics. Use real-life examples and case studies to illustrate effective marketing strategies and tactics.

Skill 28: Public Speaking

Importance:
Public speaking skills are essential for effectively communicating ideas, inspiring action, and engaging audiences in various settings, including presentations, meetings, and events. They involve confidence, clarity, and persuasion to deliver compelling speeches or presentations.

Concept:
Public speaking skills encompass the ability to structure speeches, engage audiences, manage nerves, and deliver messages effectively. They include skills such as vocal modulation, body language, storytelling, and audience interaction.

Takeaway: Guide for Students and Professionals
By mastering public speaking skills, individuals can convey their messages with confidence, influence others, and advance their personal and professional goals. Public speaking skills are valuable in roles requiring communication, leadership, and persuasion.

For a beginner student today, mastering public speaking is a valuable skill for effectively communicating ideas, inspiring others, and building confidence in various academic, professional, and personal settings. Public speaking involves delivering presentations, speeches, or talks to an audience with clarity, confidence, and impact.

Key components of public speaking skills include:

1. Preparation : Thoroughly preparing for the presentation by researching the topic, organizing the content, and creating a clear and coherent structure. This involves identifying key messages, supporting points, and relevant examples or evidence to convey the message effectively.

2. Audience Analysis : Understanding the audience's demographics, interests, and knowledge level to tailor the content and delivery to their needs and preferences. This includes considering factors such as age, background, and expectations to engage and connect with the audience effectively.

3. Confidence and Presence : Projecting confidence and enthusiasm through body language, vocal delivery, and demeanor. This includes maintaining eye contact, using gestures and facial expressions to express ideas, and speaking with a clear and audible voice.

4. Engagement and Interaction : Keeping the audience engaged and involved throughout the presentation through storytelling, humor, questions, or interactive elements. This involves establishing rapport with the audience, eliciting their participation, and responding to their reactions and feedback.

5. Clarity and Conciseness : Communicating ideas clearly and concisely to ensure understanding and retention. This includes organizing the content logically, using simple and straightforward language, and avoiding jargon or complex terminology that may confuse the audience.

6. Adaptability : Being flexible and adaptable to unexpected situations or challenges that may arise during the presentation. This involves thinking on your feet, adjusting the delivery based on audience feedback, and staying composed under pressure.

7. Visual Aids : Using visual aids, such as slides, props, or multimedia elements, to enhance the presentation and reinforce key points. Visual aids should complement the spoken words and help illustrate complex concepts or data visually.

8. Rehearsal : Practicing the presentation multiple times to refine the delivery, timing, and overall performance. This includes rehearsing in front of a mirror, recording practice sessions, or seeking feedback from peers or mentors to improve effectiveness.

9. Authenticity and Passion : Being genuine and authentic in your delivery, conveying passion and enthusiasm for the topic. Authenticity helps establish credibility and emotional connection with the audience, making the presentation more compelling and memorable.

10. Handling Q&A Sessions : Anticipating and preparing for questions from the audience by reviewing the content, anticipating potential inquiries, and formulating thoughtful responses. This includes listening carefully to questions, providing clear and concise answers, and addressing any concerns or objections respectfully.

By developing strong public speaking skills, students can enhance their ability to communicate effectively, engage with others, and influence positive change in various aspects of their lives. These skills are valuable not only for academic presentations but also for professional presentations, job interviews, networking events, and public speaking opportunities. Public speaking skills empower students to express themselves confidently, share their ideas persuasively, and make a lasting impact on others.

Ideas for Study Material/Resources:
Books: "Talk Like TED: The 9 Public-Speaking Secrets of the World's Top Minds" by Carmine Gallo, "The Art of Public Speaking" by Dale Carnegie and Joseph Berg Esenwein, "Confessions of a Public Speaker" by Scott Berkun.
Online Courses: Platforms like Udemy, Toastmasters International, and Coursera offer courses on public speaking, presentation skills, and speechwriting.
Articles and Blogs: Public speaking blogs, TED Talks, and communication websites often feature articles on public speaking tips, techniques, and inspiring speeches.

Ideas for Activity:
Conduct public speaking workshops where participants practice speech delivery, receive constructive feedback, and work on improving their presentation skills.
Organize public speaking contests or storytelling sessions where participants showcase their public speaking abilities and storytelling prowess.

Some Training Ideas for Facilitation:
Start by defining public speaking and its importance in effectively communicating ideas and influencing others.
Teach public speaking techniques, including speech structure, vocal variety, gestures, and visual aids.
Provide guidance on overcoming public speaking anxiety, handling Q&A sessions, and engaging with diverse audiences.

Did You Know?
Research shows that individuals with strong public speaking skills are perceived as more confident, credible, and persuasive, leading to increased opportunities for career advancement and leadership roles.

Ideas for Presentation:
Create a PowerPoint presentation or e-book summarizing key public speaking skills, presentation tips, and best practices. Include examples of effective speeches and techniques for overcoming public speaking anxiety.

Training Video Guide:
Develop video tutorials demonstrating various public speaking techniques, such as delivering a persuasive speech, storytelling, and handling challenging audience questions. Use real-life examples and role-plays to illustrate effective public speaking strategies and tactics.

Skill 29: Cultural Awareness

Importance:
Cultural awareness is essential for navigating diverse cultural environments, respecting differences, and building inclusive relationships. It involves understanding

cultural norms, values, beliefs, and practices to communicate effectively and avoid misunderstandings.

Concept:
Cultural awareness encompasses sensitivity to cultural differences, openness to learning about other cultures, and the ability to adapt behavior accordingly. It includes skills such as empathy, curiosity, and intercultural communication.

Takeaway: Guide for Students and Professionals
By mastering cultural awareness, individuals can foster positive interactions, build trust across cultural boundaries, and work effectively in multicultural teams. Cultural awareness is valuable in global business, international relations, and cross-cultural interactions.
Cultural awareness is crucial for students today, as it enables them to navigate diverse environments, respect different perspectives, and foster inclusive communities. Cultural awareness involves understanding, appreciating, and valuing the beliefs, customs, traditions, and norms of different cultures.

Key components of cultural awareness include:

1.   Self-Reflection : Reflecting on one's own cultural background, biases, and assumptions. This involves acknowledging one's cultural identity and recognizing how it influences perceptions, behaviors, and interactions with others.

2. Respect for Diversity : Embracing diversity and recognizing the richness of different cultures. This includes valuing cultural differences and avoiding stereotypes or judgments based on cultural background.

3.   Empathy and Perspective-Taking : Putting oneself in others' shoes and understanding their experiences, values, and perspectives. This helps foster empathy and understanding across cultural boundaries, promoting mutual respect and cooperation.

4. Cross-Cultural Communication : Developing effective communication skills across cultural contexts. This involves being mindful of cultural differences in communication styles, body language, and verbal cues, and adapting one's communication approach accordingly.

5. Cultural Sensitivity : Being aware of cultural norms, taboos, and customs when interacting with individuals from different cultures. This includes showing sensitivity to religious practices, dietary restrictions, and cultural traditions to avoid unintentional offense or misunderstanding.

6. Cultural Intelligence : Developing cultural intelligence or the ability to function effectively in diverse cultural settings. This involves being open-minded, adaptable, and willing to learn from others' perspectives, experiences, and practices.

7. Global Awareness : Understanding the interconnectedness of the world and recognizing the impact of globalization on culture, society, and the economy. This includes staying informed about global issues, trends, and events that shape the world we live in.

8. Promotion of Inclusion and Equity : Actively promoting inclusivity and equity in all aspects of life, including education, employment, and community engagement. This involves advocating for diversity initiatives, challenging discrimination, and creating spaces where everyone feels valued and respected.

9. Cultural Competence : Developing cultural competence or the ability to interact effectively with people from different cultural backgrounds. This involves acquiring knowledge about diverse cultures, building relationships across cultural boundaries, and adapting behaviors to foster positive cross-cultural interactions.

10. Lifelong Learning : Committing to continuous learning and growth in cultural awareness. This involves seeking out opportunities to engage with diverse perspectives, cultures, and experiences, both locally and globally.

By developing strong cultural awareness, students can enhance their ability to thrive in diverse and multicultural environments, build meaningful relationships with people from different backgrounds, and contribute to a more inclusive and harmonious society. Cultural awareness is a valuable skill that empowers students to navigate the complexities of our interconnected world with respect, empathy, and understanding.

Ideas for Study Material/Resources:
Books: "The Culture Map" by Erin Meyer, "Cultural Intelligence: Living and Working Globally" by David C. Thomas and Kerr C. Inkson, "When Cultures Collide: Leading Across Cultures" by Richard D. Lewis.
Online Courses: Platforms like Coursera, Cultural Detective, and Global Competence Certificate offer courses on cultural competence, diversity, and inclusion.
Articles and Blogs: Cross-cultural communication websites, intercultural training blogs, and diversity publications often feature articles on cultural awareness, multiculturalism, and global perspectives.

Ideas for Activity:
Conduct cultural sensitivity workshops where participants explore cultural dimensions, discuss case studies, and practice cross-cultural communication.
Organize cultural immersion experiences or international exchange programs where participants engage with diverse cultures firsthand and reflect on their experiences.

Some Training Ideas for Facilitation:
Start by defining cultural awareness and its importance in fostering inclusivity, respect, and understanding.
Teach cultural dimensions, such as Hofstede's cultural dimensions theory, and their impact on communication styles, decision-making processes, and workplace dynamics.

Provide guidance on building cultural competence, including active listening, empathy, adapting communication styles, and resolving cultural conflicts.

Did You Know?
Research shows that culturally diverse teams outperform homogeneous teams when they effectively leverage their cultural differences and capitalize on diverse perspectives and talents.

Ideas for Presentation:
Create a PowerPoint presentation or e-book summarizing key cultural awareness concepts, cultural dimensions, and best practices for effective intercultural communication. Include case studies and examples to illustrate successful cross-cultural interactions.

Training Video Guide:
Develop video tutorials demonstrating various cultural awareness techniques, such as navigating cultural differences, adapting communication styles, and building rapport across cultures. Use real-life examples and cultural scenarios to illustrate effective cross-cultural communication strategies and skills.

Skill 30: Team Management

Importance:
Team management skills are essential for leading, motivating, and developing teams to achieve common goals and deliver results. They involve leadership, communication, and interpersonal skills to build high-performing teams and foster collaboration.

Concept:
Team management encompasses the ability to set clear goals, delegate tasks, provide feedback, and resolve conflicts within teams. It includes skills such as coaching, mentoring, and empowering team members to reach their full potential.

Takeaway: Guide for Students and Professionals
By mastering team management skills, individuals can effectively lead teams, improve team performance, and create a positive work environment. Team management is critical for project success, organizational productivity, and employee engagement.
For a beginner student today, mastering team management skills is essential for effectively leading and collaborating with others in academic, professional, and personal settings. Team management involves coordinating and guiding individuals towards achieving common goals, fostering teamwork, and maximizing collective performance.

Key components of team management skills include:

1. Effective Communication : Developing strong communication skills to convey ideas clearly, listen actively to team members' input, and provide feedback. Clear and open

communication fosters understanding, resolves conflicts, and builds trust within the team.

2. Goal Setting and Planning : Establishing clear goals, objectives, and timelines for the team's projects or tasks. This involves defining roles and responsibilities, allocating resources, and creating action plans to achieve desired outcomes.

3. Team Building : Creating a positive and cohesive team culture that promotes collaboration, mutual respect, and camaraderie. This includes fostering a sense of belonging, recognizing individual strengths, and celebrating achievements together.

4. Conflict Resolution : Developing strategies for addressing conflicts and resolving disagreements within the team. This involves facilitating constructive dialogue, finding common ground, and seeking win-win solutions that benefit everyone involved.

5. Delegation : Assigning tasks and responsibilities to team members based on their skills, strengths, and interests. Effective delegation empowers team members, distributes workload evenly, and allows for efficient use of resources.

6. Motivation and Engagement : Inspiring and motivating team members to perform at their best and stay committed to the team's goals. This may involve providing recognition, rewards, and opportunities for growth, as well as fostering a supportive and encouraging environment.

7. Decision Making : Facilitating decision-making processes within the team, whether through consensus-building, democratic voting, or other methods. This involves weighing various options, considering different perspectives, and making informed decisions that align with the team's objectives.

8. Performance Management : Monitoring and evaluating team performance against established goals and benchmarks. This includes providing regular feedback, identifying areas for improvement, and implementing strategies to enhance performance and productivity.

9. Adaptability and Flexibility : Being adaptable and flexible in response to changing circumstances, priorities, and challenges. This involves adjusting plans, reallocating resources, and revising strategies as needed to ensure the team remains effective and resilient.

10. Empowerment and Development : Empowering team members to take ownership of their work, develop new skills, and grow professionally. This includes providing opportunities for learning and development, mentoring, and coaching to support individual and collective growth.

By developing strong team management skills, students can enhance their ability to lead, collaborate, and succeed in group settings. These skills are valuable not only for academic projects and extracurricular activities but also for future careers in management, leadership, and teamwork-oriented professions. Effective team management empowers students to harness the collective talents and strengths of a group to achieve common goals and drive positive outcomes.

Ideas for Study Material/Resources:
Books: "The Five Dysfunctions of a Team" by Patrick Lencioni, "Leaders Eat Last" by Simon Sinek, "High Output Management" by Andrew S. Grove.
Online Courses: Platforms like LinkedIn Learning, Harvard Business School Online, and Udemy offer courses on team leadership, performance management, and conflict resolution.
Articles and Blogs: Team management blogs, leadership publications, and management websites often feature articles on team dynamics, leadership styles, and effective team-building strategies.

Ideas for Activity:
Conduct team-building workshops where participants engage in collaborative activities, problem-solving challenges, and trust-building exercises.
Facilitate team meetings or brainstorming sessions where participants work together to solve real-world problems or generate innovative ideas.

Some Training Ideas for Facilitation:
Start by defining team management and its importance in driving team performance and achieving organizational objectives.
Teach team leadership principles, including setting clear expectations, fostering trust, promoting accountability, and recognizing team achievements.
Provide guidance on building cohesive teams, managing team dynamics, and resolving conflicts constructively.

Did You Know?
Research shows that effective team management can lead to higher team morale, lower turnover rates, and increased productivity, resulting in better organizational outcomes and employee satisfaction.

Ideas for Presentation:
Create a PowerPoint presentation or e-book summarizing key team management concepts, team leadership strategies, and best practices. Include case studies and examples to illustrate successful team management approaches.

Training Video Guide:
Develop video tutorials demonstrating various team management techniques, such as conducting team meetings, providing constructive feedback, and fostering team collaboration. Use real-life examples and team scenarios to illustrate effective team management skills and practices.

Skill 31: Active Listening

Importance:
Active listening is crucial for building rapport, understanding others' perspectives, and fostering effective communication. It involves giving full attention to the speaker, processing their message, and responding appropriately.

Concept:
Active listening encompasses techniques such as maintaining eye contact, nodding, paraphrasing, and asking clarifying questions to demonstrate understanding and empathy. It involves withholding judgment and focusing on the speaker's message.

Takeaway: Guide for Students and Professionals
By mastering active listening skills, individuals can improve their relationships, resolve conflicts, and collaborate more effectively. Active listening fosters trust, mutual respect, and open communication in both personal and professional settings.
Active listening is a foundational skill for students, enabling them to engage more deeply in academic discussions, understand complex concepts, and build stronger relationships with peers and instructors. Active listening goes beyond simply hearing words; it involves fully concentrating on what is being said, understanding the message, and responding thoughtfully.

Key components of active listening include:

1. Attention and Focus : Paying full attention to the speaker and avoiding distractions. This means putting away electronic devices, making eye contact, and maintaining an open posture to signal interest and attentiveness.

2. Empathy and Understanding : Putting oneself in the speaker's shoes and trying to see things from their perspective. This involves listening with empathy, acknowledging the speaker's feelings, and validating their experiences.

3. Nonverbal Cues : Paying attention to the speaker's body language, facial expressions, and tone of voice to understand the underlying emotions and context of the message. Nonverbal cues often convey additional information that complements verbal communication.

4. Clarification and Confirmation : Asking questions or providing feedback to ensure understanding and clarity. This may involve paraphrasing the speaker's message, summarizing key points, or asking for examples to confirm comprehension.

5. Suspending Judgment : Avoiding premature judgment or evaluation of the speaker's ideas or opinions. Active listeners withhold their own assumptions or biases and remain open-minded to new perspectives and insights.

6. Respectful Silence : Allowing moments of silence for reflection and processing of information. Silence provides space for the speaker to express themselves fully and for the listener to absorb and digest the message.

7. Reflective Responses : Responding to the speaker in a way that demonstrates understanding and validation. This may involve offering empathetic statements, affirming the speaker's feelings, or providing encouragement and support.

8. Summarization : Summarizing the main points of the speaker's message to demonstrate active engagement and to clarify understanding. Summarization helps to reinforce key ideas and ensure that both parties are on the same page.

9. Feedback and Follow-Up : Providing constructive feedback or follow-up questions to deepen the conversation and address any areas of confusion or disagreement. Feedback helps to enhance mutual understanding and build rapport between the speaker and listener.

10. Practice and Reflection : Practicing active listening regularly and reflecting on one's listening habits and skills. Like any skill, active listening improves with practice and self-awareness, leading to more effective communication and deeper connections with others.

By developing strong active listening skills, students can enhance their ability to learn from lectures, participate actively in discussions, and collaborate effectively with peers. Active listening also fosters empathy, respect, and understanding in interpersonal relationships, contributing to a positive and supportive learning environment.

Ideas for Study Material/Resources:
Books: "The Lost Art of Listening" by Michael P. Nichols, "Just Listen" by Mark Goulston, "You're Not Listening" by Kate Murphy.
Online Courses: Platforms like Coursera, LinkedIn Learning, and Udemy offer courses on active listening, communication skills, and interpersonal effectiveness.
Articles and Blogs: Communication blogs, psychology websites, and coaching platforms often feature articles on active listening techniques, benefits, and case studies.

Ideas for Activity:
Conduct active listening exercises where participants pair up and take turns sharing their thoughts and experiences while the other practices active listening techniques.
Facilitate group discussions or role-plays where participants practice active listening skills in various scenarios, such as conflict resolution or customer service interactions.

Some Training Ideas for Facilitation:
Start by defining active listening and its importance in effective communication and relationship-building.
Teach active listening techniques, including non-verbal cues, reflective listening, summarizing, and empathetic responses.

Provide opportunities for participants to practice active listening in simulated and real-life situations, with feedback and reflection.

Did You Know?
Research shows that active listening can improve job performance, enhance leadership effectiveness, and reduce misunderstandings and conflicts in teams and organizations.

Ideas for Presentation:
Create a PowerPoint presentation or e-book summarizing key active listening techniques, benefits, and strategies for improving listening skills. Include scenarios and examples to illustrate effective active listening in various contexts.

Training Video Guide:
Develop video tutorials demonstrating various active listening techniques, such as paraphrasing, reflecting feelings, and maintaining eye contact. Use role-plays and real-life scenarios to illustrate effective active listening skills and their impact on communication.

Skill 32: Coaching and Mentoring

Importance:
Coaching and mentoring skills are essential for developing others, fostering learning and growth, and building a supportive work culture. They involve providing guidance, feedback, and encouragement to help individuals achieve their goals and reach their full potential.

Concept:
Coaching and mentoring encompass the ability to assess individuals' strengths and development areas, set goals, provide constructive feedback, and offer support and resources for learning and improvement. They require empathy, patience, and effective communication skills.

Takeaway: Guide for Students and Professionals
By mastering coaching and mentoring skills, individuals can empower others, enhance team performance, and cultivate a culture of continuous learning and development. Coaching and mentoring are valuable for leadership development, talent retention, and succession planning.
Coaching and mentoring are invaluable skills for students to develop, as they facilitate personal and professional growth, support learning, and foster positive relationships. Both coaching and mentoring involve guiding and supporting individuals to achieve their goals, but they differ in their focus and approach.

Key components of coaching and mentoring skills include:

1. Establishing Trust and Rapport : Building a trusting relationship with the individual being coached or mentored is essential for effective guidance and support. This involves creating a safe and supportive environment where the individual feels comfortable sharing their goals, challenges, and aspirations.

2. Active Listening : Practicing active listening to understand the individual's needs, concerns, and aspirations fully. This involves paying attention, asking probing questions, and demonstrating empathy to gain insights into the individual's perspectives and experiences.

3. Setting Clear Goals and Expectations : Clarifying the individual's goals, expectations, and desired outcomes for the coaching or mentoring relationship. This involves collaboratively setting SMART (Specific, Measurable, Achievable, Relevant, Time-bound) goals that align with the individual's aspirations and development needs.

4. Providing Constructive Feedback : Offering feedback and constructive criticism in a supportive and non-judgmental manner. Feedback should be specific, actionable, and focused on helping the individual identify areas for improvement and grow professionally and personally.

5. Supporting Development and Growth : Providing guidance, resources, and opportunities for the individual to develop their skills, knowledge, and capabilities. This may involve sharing expertise, offering advice, and facilitating learning experiences that support the individual's development goals.

6. Coaching and Mentoring Techniques : Employing a variety of coaching and mentoring techniques, such as goal setting, action planning, role-playing, and reflective questioning. These techniques help to stimulate learning, promote self-awareness, and empower the individual to take ownership of their development.

7. Building Confidence and Self-Efficacy : Encouraging and empowering the individual to believe in their abilities and potential. This involves acknowledging their strengths, celebrating successes, and providing support and encouragement during times of challenge or self-doubt.

8. Promoting Accountability and Responsibility : Holding the individual accountable for their actions, commitments, and progress towards their goals. This involves setting milestones, tracking progress, and providing gentle reminders to help the individual stay focused and motivated.

9. Flexibility and Adaptability : Being flexible and adaptable in coaching or mentoring approaches to meet the individual's unique needs and preferences. This may involve adjusting communication styles, pacing, or content delivery to accommodate different learning styles and personalities.

10. Ethical Considerations : Upholding ethical principles and maintaining confidentiality, integrity, and professionalism in coaching or mentoring relationships.

This includes respecting boundaries, avoiding conflicts of interest, and prioritizing the individual's best interests.

By developing strong coaching and mentoring skills, students can enhance their ability to support and empower others, contribute positively to their personal and professional development, and foster a culture of learning and growth. Coaching and mentoring skills are valuable not only for future leadership roles but also for building strong interpersonal relationships and making a positive impact in various contexts.

Ideas for Study Material/Resources:
Books: "The Coaching Habit" by Michael Bungay Stanier, "The Mentor's Guide" by Lois J. Zachary, "Coaching for Performance" by John Whitmore.
Online Courses: Platforms like Udemy, Coursera, and CoachU offer courses on coaching skills, mentorship, and leadership development.
Articles and Blogs: Coaching websites, leadership blogs, and HR publications often feature articles on coaching and mentoring best practices, case studies, and success stories.

Ideas for Activity:
Organize coaching circles or peer coaching sessions where participants take turns coaching and receiving feedback from each other on specific goals or challenges.
Pair participants with mentors or mentees and facilitate regular meetings or check-ins to discuss progress, share insights, and provide support.

Some Training Ideas for Facilitation:
Start by defining coaching and mentoring and their role in personal and professional development.
Teach coaching and mentoring techniques, including active listening, asking powerful questions, providing constructive feedback, and setting SMART goals.
Provide opportunities for participants to practice coaching and mentoring skills through role-plays, case studies, and real-life coaching conversations.

Did You Know?
Research shows that organizations with strong coaching and mentoring cultures have higher employee engagement, retention, and performance levels.

Ideas for Presentation:
Create a PowerPoint presentation or e-book summarizing key coaching and mentoring concepts, techniques, and best practices. Include case studies and examples to illustrate successful coaching and mentoring relationships.

Training Video Guide:
Develop video tutorials demonstrating various coaching and mentoring techniques, such as active listening, goal setting, and providing constructive feedback. Use role-plays and real-life scenarios to illustrate effective coaching and mentoring interactions and outcomes.

Skill 33: Persuasion Skills

Importance:
Persuasion skills are crucial for influencing others, gaining buy-in for ideas or proposals, and driving action. They involve understanding motivations, presenting compelling arguments, and building trust to persuade others to adopt a particular viewpoint or take a desired course of action.

Concept:
Persuasion skills encompass techniques such as storytelling, logical reasoning, emotional appeal, and social proof to effectively communicate messages and change attitudes or behaviors. They require empathy, credibility, and adaptability to resonate with different audiences.

Takeaway: Guide for Students and Professionals
By mastering persuasion skills, individuals can negotiate effectively, sell products or services, and rally support for initiatives or projects. Persuasion skills are valuable for leaders, sales professionals, marketers, and anyone seeking to influence others positively.
Persuasion skills are vital for students to master as they navigate academic assignments, social interactions, and future careers. These skills enable students to influence others' beliefs, attitudes, and behaviors effectively, fostering collaboration, negotiation, and decision-making.

Key components of persuasion skills include:

1. Understanding Persuasion Principles : Familiarizing oneself with the principles of persuasion, such as reciprocity, social proof, authority, consistency, liking, and scarcity. Understanding these principles helps students develop persuasive messages and strategies that resonate with their audience.

2. Knowing the Audience : Understanding the needs, preferences, and motivations of the target audience. This involves conducting audience analysis to identify their values, beliefs, and concerns, allowing students to tailor their persuasive appeals accordingly.

3. Building Credibility : Establishing credibility and trustworthiness to enhance the persuasiveness of one's message. This may involve showcasing expertise, providing evidence or testimonials, and demonstrating sincerity and authenticity in communication.

4. Crafting Compelling Messages : Developing persuasive messages that are clear, concise, and compelling. This includes structuring messages with a strong introduction, supporting arguments, and a persuasive conclusion, as well as using persuasive language and storytelling techniques to engage the audience emotionally.

5. Using Persuasive Techniques : Employing various persuasive techniques, such as rhetorical devices, analogies, metaphors, and vivid imagery, to captivate the audience's attention and stimulate their emotions. These techniques help make the message more memorable and persuasive.

6. Addressing Counterarguments : Anticipating and addressing potential objections or counterarguments to one's message. This involves acknowledging opposing viewpoints, providing counterarguments or rebuttals, and offering evidence or examples to support one's position.

7. Active Listening and Empathy : Demonstrating empathy and active listening to understand the audience's perspective and concerns. This allows students to tailor their persuasive appeals to address the audience's needs and interests effectively.

8. Building Relationships : Cultivating positive relationships with the audience to increase receptiveness to persuasion. This involves establishing rapport, demonstrating genuine interest and concern, and showing respect for the audience's opinions and experiences.

9. Negotiation and Compromise : Employing negotiation skills to find common ground and reach mutually beneficial agreements. This involves being flexible, open-minded, and willing to compromise to achieve shared objectives.

10. Ethical Considerations : Upholding ethical principles and integrity in persuasion efforts. This includes being honest and transparent in communication, avoiding manipulation or coercion, and respecting the autonomy and dignity of others.

By developing strong persuasion skills, students can enhance their ability to influence others positively, advocate for their ideas, and achieve their goals effectively. These skills are valuable not only for academic success but also for navigating social interactions, professional settings, and leadership roles. Persuasion skills empower students to communicate persuasively, build relationships, and make a meaningful impact in various aspects of their lives.

Ideas for Study Material/Resources:
Books: "Influence: The Psychology of Persuasion" by Robert B. Cialdini, "Yes!: 50 Scientifically Proven Ways to Be Persuasive" by Noah J. Goldstein, Steve J. Martin, and Robert B. Cialdini, "To Sell is Human" by Daniel H. Pink.
Online Courses: Platforms like Coursera, LinkedIn Learning, and MasterClass offer courses on persuasion techniques, negotiation skills, and influence strategies.
Articles and Blogs: Psychology Today, Harvard Business Review, and Forbes often feature articles on persuasion psychology, sales tactics, and communication strategies.

Ideas for Activity:
Conduct persuasive speaking contests or debates where participants present arguments and counterarguments on a given topic and persuade the audience to support their viewpoint.

Organize role-playing exercises where participants take on different roles (e.g., salesperson, negotiator, influencer) and practice applying persuasion techniques in various scenarios.

Some Training Ideas for Facilitation:
Start by defining persuasion skills and their importance in influencing others positively and achieving desired outcomes.
Teach persuasion principles, including reciprocity, scarcity, authority, consistency, liking, and social proof, as outlined in Robert Cialdini's six principles of influence.
Provide guidance on crafting persuasive messages, understanding audience needs and motivations, and adapting persuasion strategies to different situations and personalities.

Did You Know?
Research shows that individuals with strong persuasion skills are more effective communicators, negotiators, and leaders, leading to better outcomes in personal and professional contexts.

Ideas for Presentation:
Create a PowerPoint presentation or e-book summarizing key persuasion concepts, techniques, and strategies for influencing others positively. Include case studies and examples to illustrate successful persuasion campaigns and tactics.

Training Video Guide:
Develop video tutorials demonstrating various persuasion techniques, such as storytelling, framing, and using persuasive language. Use real-life examples and scenarios to illustrate effective persuasion strategies and their impact on decision-making.

Skill 34: Goal Setting and Achievement

Importance:
Goal setting and achievement skills are essential for clarifying objectives, staying focused, and taking consistent action to accomplish desired outcomes. They involve setting SMART (Specific, Measurable, Achievable, Relevant, Time-bound) goals, developing action plans, and monitoring progress to achieve success.

Concept:
Goal setting and achievement encompass the process of defining clear and achievable goals, breaking them down into manageable tasks, and taking systematic steps to accomplish them. They require self-awareness, motivation, and resilience to overcome obstacles and stay committed to goals.

Takeaway: Guide for Students and Professionals
By mastering goal setting and achievement skills, individuals can increase productivity, improve performance, and experience a sense of fulfillment and satisfaction. Goal

setting is fundamental to personal development, career advancement, and lifelong learning.

Goal setting and achievement are fundamental skills for students to develop, enabling them to clarify objectives, stay motivated, and track progress towards success. Effective goal setting involves defining specific, measurable, achievable, relevant, and time-bound (SMART) goals and implementing strategies to achieve them.

Key components of goal setting and achievement skills include:

1. Clarity and Specificity : Clearly defining goals that are specific, measurable, and actionable. This involves identifying what students want to achieve, breaking down larger goals into smaller, manageable tasks, and establishing clear criteria for success.

2. Relevance and Alignment : Ensuring that goals are relevant to students' values, aspirations, and long-term objectives. Goals should align with students' personal interests, academic pursuits, and career ambitions to maintain motivation and commitment.

3. Achievability and Realism : Setting goals that are challenging yet attainable within a reasonable timeframe. This involves considering students' abilities, resources, and constraints, as well as assessing potential obstacles and developing strategies to overcome them.

4. Time-Bound : Establishing deadlines or timelines for achieving goals to create a sense of urgency and accountability. Breaking down goals into smaller, time-bound milestones helps students track progress and stay focused on their objectives.

5. Action Planning : Developing action plans that outline the specific steps, tasks, and resources required to achieve goals. This involves identifying necessary actions, setting priorities, and creating a roadmap for implementation.

6. Monitoring and Evaluation : Regularly monitoring progress towards goals and evaluating outcomes against predetermined criteria. This includes tracking key performance indicators (KPIs), assessing strengths and weaknesses, and adjusting strategies as needed to stay on track.

7. Flexibility and Adaptability : Being flexible and adaptable in response to changing circumstances, setbacks, or unexpected challenges. This involves revising goals, modifying action plans, and exploring alternative approaches to achieve desired outcomes.

8. Motivation and Persistence : Maintaining motivation and persistence in pursuit of goals, especially during times of difficulty or adversity. This includes staying focused on the end result, celebrating small victories along the way, and cultivating a growth mindset that embraces challenges as opportunities for learning and growth.

9. Self-Reflection and Adjustment : Engaging in regular self-reflection to assess progress, identify barriers, and adjust strategies as needed. This involves being honest

with oneself about strengths and weaknesses, seeking feedback from others, and learning from past experiences to improve future performance.

10.   Celebrating Achievements : Celebrating successes and milestones along the journey towards goal attainment. Recognizing achievements, no matter how small, helps reinforce positive behaviors, boost confidence, and maintain momentum towards future goals.

By developing strong goal setting and achievement skills, students can enhance their ability to set meaningful objectives, take proactive steps towards realizing them, and experience a sense of fulfillment and accomplishment in their academic and personal lives. These skills are essential for fostering self-directed learning, promoting personal growth, and achieving success in both short-term tasks and long-term aspirations.

Ideas for Study Material/Resources:
Books: "Goals!: How to Get Everything You Want—Faster Than You Ever Thought Possible" by Brian Tracy, "The 12 Week Year" by Brian P. Moran and Michael Lennington, "Atomic Habits" by James Clear.
Online Courses: Platforms like Coursera, Udemy, and MindTools offer courses on goal setting, productivity, and personal development.
Articles and Blogs: Productivity blogs, personal development websites, and self-help publications often feature articles on goal setting strategies, time management, and habit formation.

Ideas for Activity:
Conduct goal-setting workshops where participants identify their long-term objectives, break them down into actionable steps, and create SMART goals for different areas of their lives.
Organize accountability groups or buddy systems where participants support each other in setting and achieving goals, providing encouragement, and holding each other accountable.

Some Training Ideas for Facilitation:
Start by defining goal setting and its importance in personal and professional success. Teach goal-setting principles, including specificity, measurability, achievability, relevance, and time-bound nature of goals (SMART criteria).
Provide guidance on developing action plans, prioritizing tasks, tracking progress, and adjusting goals as needed to stay on track.

Did You Know?
Research shows that individuals who set specific goals are more likely to achieve them compared to those with vague or undefined goals.

Ideas for Presentation:
Create a PowerPoint presentation or e-book summarizing key goal-setting concepts, techniques, and best practices. Include templates and worksheets to help participants set and track their goals effectively.

Training Video Guide:
Develop video tutorials demonstrating various goal-setting techniques, such as vision boarding, mind mapping, and using productivity tools. Use real-life examples and success stories to illustrate effective goal-setting strategies and their impact on personal and professional growth.

Skill 35: AI Tools

Importance:
Proficiency in using AI tools is becoming increasingly important in various fields, including data analysis, automation, and decision-making. AI tools can streamline processes, analyze large datasets, and generate insights to drive innovation and efficiency.

Concept:
AI tools encompass a wide range of technologies and applications, including machine learning, natural language processing, computer vision, and robotic process automation. They enable computers to perform tasks that typically require human intelligence, such as learning from data, recognizing patterns, and making predictions.

Takeaway: Guide for Students and Professionals
By mastering AI tools, individuals can enhance their productivity, make data-driven decisions, and leverage technology to gain a competitive edge. AI skills are in high demand across industries, offering opportunities for career advancement and professional growth.
AI tools encompass a wide range of applications that leverage artificial intelligence (AI) technologies to perform tasks autonomously or assist humans in various activities. These tools are designed to analyze data, make predictions, automate processes, and enhance decision-making across different domains.

Key categories of AI tools include:

1. Natural Language Processing (NLP) :
  - NLP tools analyze and understand human language, enabling tasks such as text analysis, sentiment analysis, language translation, and chatbot interactions.
  - Examples: Google Cloud Natural Language API, IBM Watson NLP, NLTK (Natural Language Toolkit), spaCy.

2. Machine Learning (ML) :
  - ML tools use algorithms and statistical models to analyze data, identify patterns, and make predictions without explicit programming instructions.
  - Examples: TensorFlow, PyTorch, scikit-learn, Keras, Microsoft Azure Machine Learning.

3. Computer Vision :

- Computer vision tools process and interpret visual information from images or videos, enabling tasks such as object detection, image classification, facial recognition, and image generation.
- Examples: OpenCV, TensorFlow Object Detection API, Amazon Rekognition, Microsoft Azure Computer Vision.

4. Speech Recognition :
- Speech recognition tools convert spoken language into text, enabling tasks such as voice commands, speech-to-text transcription, and voice-enabled interfaces.
- Examples: Google Speech-to-Text API, IBM Watson Speech to Text, Microsoft Azure Speech Service, Mozilla DeepSpeech.

5. Robotic Process Automation (RPA) :
- RPA tools automate repetitive and rule-based tasks by emulating human interactions with digital systems, leading to increased efficiency and productivity.
- Examples: UiPath, Automation Anywhere, Blue Prism, Microsoft Power Automate.

6. Data Analytics and Business Intelligence :
- Data analytics and BI tools analyze large datasets to uncover insights, trends, and patterns that inform business decisions and strategies.
- Examples: Tableau, Microsoft Power BI, Google Data Studio, QlikView, Domo.

7. Recommendation Systems :
- Recommendation systems analyze user preferences and behavior to provide personalized recommendations for products, content, or services.
- Examples: Amazon Personalize, Netflix recommendation algorithm, Spotify Discover Weekly, Google Recommendations AI.

8. Virtual Assistants :
- Virtual assistants are AI-powered software agents designed to assist users with tasks, answer questions, schedule appointments, and provide information through voice or text interfaces.
- Examples: Amazon Alexa, Apple Siri, Google Assistant, Microsoft Cortana.

9. Deep Learning :
- Deep learning tools use artificial neural networks with multiple layers to learn complex patterns and representations from data, enabling advanced applications in image recognition, speech synthesis, and natural language understanding.
- Examples: DeepMind, NVIDIA CUDA Toolkit, Apache MXNet, Hugging Face Transformers.

10. AI Development Frameworks and Libraries :
- AI development frameworks and libraries provide tools and resources for building, training, and deploying AI models across various domains and platforms.
- Examples: TensorFlow, PyTorch, Keras, Apache Spark MLlib, Microsoft Cognitive Toolkit.

These AI tools empower users to harness the capabilities of artificial intelligence for solving complex problems, optimizing processes, and unlocking new opportunities for innovation and advancement across industries and domains.

Ideas for Study Material/Resources:
Books: "Hands-On Machine Learning with Scikit-Learn, Keras, and TensorFlow" by Aurélien Géron, "Artificial Intelligence: A Guide for Thinking Humans" by Melanie Mitchell, "Deep Learning" by Ian Goodfellow, Yoshua Bengio, and Aaron Courville.
Online Courses: Platforms like Coursera, edX, and Udacity offer courses on AI, machine learning, and deep learning, often taught by leading experts in the field.
Articles and Blogs: AI research papers, tech blogs, and industry publications such as Towards Data Science and AI Weekly feature articles on AI tools, algorithms, and applications.

Ideas for Activity:
Conduct hands-on workshops where participants explore AI tools and platforms, such as TensorFlow, PyTorch, or Google Cloud AI, through guided tutorials and exercises.
Organize hackathons or data analysis competitions where participants use AI tools to solve real-world problems or analyze datasets to extract insights.

Some Training Ideas for Facilitation:
Start by providing an overview of AI tools and their applications in various domains, from image recognition to natural language processing.
Teach fundamental concepts of machine learning, neural networks, and deep learning, along with practical skills for using AI libraries and frameworks.
Provide hands-on experience with AI tools through interactive sessions, coding exercises, and real-world projects to reinforce learning and skill development.

Did You Know?
The global AI software market is projected to reach over $126 billion by 2025, reflecting the growing adoption of AI technologies across industries and sectors.

Ideas for Presentation:
Create a PowerPoint presentation or e-book summarizing key AI concepts, algorithms, and tools, along with practical tips for using AI in various applications. Include demos, code snippets, and case studies to illustrate AI techniques and their potential impact.

Training Video Guide:
Develop video tutorials demonstrating how to use specific AI tools and platforms, such as building and training neural networks, implementing machine learning algorithms, and deploying AI models in real-world scenarios. Provide step-by-step guidance and examples to help learners understand and apply AI techniques effectively.

Skill 36: Audio Editing Skills

Importance:
Audio editing skills are essential for creating high-quality audio content, such as podcasts, music, and soundtracks, with professional polish and clarity. They involve techniques for recording, editing, mixing, and mastering audio recordings to achieve desired results.

Concept:
Audio editing encompasses the manipulation of sound recordings using digital audio workstations (DAWs) and editing software. It includes tasks such as removing noise, adjusting volume levels, adding effects, and combining multiple audio tracks to create a cohesive and engaging listening experience.

Takeaway: Guide for Students and Professionals
By mastering audio editing skills, individuals can produce professional-grade audio content, enhance the clarity and quality of recordings, and express their creativity through sound. Audio editing skills are valuable for content creators, musicians, podcasters, and audio engineers.

Audio editing skills are valuable for students interested in media production, music, podcasting, and various multimedia projects. These skills involve manipulating and enhancing audio recordings to achieve desired outcomes, whether it's for professional projects or personal creative endeavors.

Key components of audio editing skills include:

1. Familiarity with Audio Editing Software : Becoming proficient in using audio editing software such as Adobe Audition, Audacity, GarageBand, Pro Tools, or Logic Pro X. Understanding the interface, tools, and features of the software is essential for efficient editing.

2. Importing and Exporting Audio Files : Knowing how to import audio files from different sources, such as recordings, music tracks, or sound effects libraries, into the editing software. Similarly, learning to export edited audio files in various formats suitable for different platforms and purposes.

3. Basic Editing Techniques : Mastering basic editing techniques such as cutting, copying, pasting, trimming, and splitting audio clips. These techniques allow students to remove unwanted sections, rearrange segments, and refine the timing of audio recordings.

4. Volume and Gain Control : Adjusting the volume levels and gain of audio clips to ensure consistent sound quality and prevent clipping or distortion. This involves using volume sliders, normalization tools, and compression techniques to balance audio levels.

5. Equalization (EQ) : Understanding how to use EQ to adjust the frequency balance of audio recordings. EQ allows students to enhance or reduce specific frequencies, such as boosting bass or treble, to improve clarity, warmth, or presence in the audio.

6. Noise Reduction and Restoration : Removing background noise, hums, clicks, pops, and other unwanted artifacts from audio recordings. This involves using noise reduction tools, spectral editing, and audio restoration techniques to clean up audio and improve its quality.

7. Effects and Processing : Applying audio effects and processing to enhance the sound or create artistic effects. This includes adding reverb, delay, chorus, flanger, or distortion effects, as well as adjusting parameters such as pitch, tempo, or modulation.

8. Fades and Crossfades : Creating smooth transitions between audio clips using fade-in, fade-out, and crossfade techniques. Fades help eliminate abrupt starts or endings and create a more polished and professional sound.

9. Mixing and Balancing : Mixing multiple audio tracks together to create a cohesive and balanced sound. This involves adjusting the volume, panning, and EQ of individual tracks to achieve a harmonious blend and spatial separation.

10. Mastering : Finalizing the audio mix and preparing it for distribution or publication. Mastering involves optimizing the overall sound quality, ensuring consistency across tracks, and applying final touches such as limiting, compression, and peak normalization.

By developing strong audio editing skills, students can produce high-quality audio content for a variety of purposes, including podcasts, music production, voiceovers, sound design, and multimedia projects. These skills enable students to express their creativity, tell compelling stories, and engage audiences through the power of sound.

Ideas for Study Material/Resources:
Books: "The Mixing Engineer's Handbook" by Bobby Owsinski, "The Audio Expert" by Ethan Winer, "Podcast Launch" by John Lee Dumas.
Online Courses: Platforms like Skillshare, Lynda.com, and Udemy offer courses on audio editing, mixing, and mastering, covering various DAWs and software tools.
Articles and Blogs: Audio engineering forums, music production blogs, and podcasting websites often feature articles on audio editing techniques, best practices, and software reviews.

Ideas for Activity:
Conduct hands-on workshops where participants learn basic audio editing techniques, such as noise reduction, equalization, and compression, using popular DAWs like Audacity, Adobe Audition, or GarageBand.
Organize collaborative projects where participants work together to edit and produce audio content, such as podcasts, interviews, or music tracks, applying advanced editing techniques and creative effects.

Some Training Ideas for Facilitation:
Start by introducing participants to the fundamentals of audio editing, including audio formats, file management, and basic editing tools and techniques.
Teach advanced audio editing skills, such as time-stretching, pitch correction, layering, and automation, along with best practices for achieving professional-quality results.
Provide hands-on practice opportunities and constructive feedback to help participants develop their audio editing skills and creative instincts.

Did You Know?
Audio editing software has democratized the creation of audio content, enabling individuals to produce professional-quality recordings from the comfort of their homes or studios.

Ideas for Presentation:
Create a PowerPoint presentation or e-book summarizing key audio editing concepts, techniques, and software tools, along with practical tips for achieving professional results. Include audio demos, tutorials, and workflow examples to illustrate different aspects of audio editing.

Training Video Guide:
Develop video tutorials demonstrating how to perform specific audio editing tasks, such as cleaning up audio recordings, applying effects, and mixing tracks. Provide step-by-step instructions and real-time demonstrations using popular DAWs and editing software to help learners visualize and understand the editing process.

Skill 37: Writing Skills

Importance:
Writing skills are essential for clear communication, effective storytelling, and conveying ideas convincingly in various formats, including emails, reports, articles, and creative works. Strong writing skills can enhance professional credibility, foster connections, and influence others positively.

Concept:
Writing skills encompass the ability to organize thoughts logically, craft coherent sentences, and choose appropriate language and tone for the audience and purpose. They involve techniques for structuring documents, refining language, and editing for clarity and impact.

Takeaway: Guide for Students and Professionals
By mastering writing skills, individuals can express themselves articulately, persuade others convincingly, and convey complex ideas with clarity and precision. Writing skills are valuable in virtually every profession and can contribute to career advancement and personal development.
Writing skills are essential for students across various academic disciplines and professional fields, enabling effective communication, critical thinking, and expression

of ideas. Strong writing skills encompass a range of abilities, from grammar and punctuation to organization and creativity.

Key components of writing skills include:

1. Grammar and Punctuation : Mastering the rules of grammar and punctuation to ensure clarity and accuracy in writing. This includes understanding sentence structure, verb tense, subject-verb agreement, punctuation marks, and proper use of capitalization.

2. Vocabulary and Word Choice : Expanding vocabulary and choosing appropriate words to convey ideas effectively. This involves using precise language, avoiding jargon or slang, and incorporating varied vocabulary to enhance the richness and clarity of writing.

3. Sentence Structure and Fluency : Crafting well-structured sentences that flow smoothly and logically. This includes varying sentence length and structure, using transitions to connect ideas, and maintaining coherence and cohesion throughout the writing.

4. Organization and Structure : Organizing ideas in a logical and coherent manner to create a clear and cohesive structure. This involves outlining main points, arranging information in a logical sequence, and using headings or subheadings to guide readers through the text.

5. Clarity and Conciseness : Writing with clarity and conciseness to convey ideas succinctly and effectively. This includes avoiding unnecessary repetition, eliminating vague or ambiguous language, and using active voice to enhance readability.

6. Audience Awareness : Tailoring writing to the needs and expectations of the intended audience. This involves considering audience demographics, background knowledge, and interests, and adjusting tone, style, and level of detail accordingly.

7. Critical Thinking and Analysis : Developing critical thinking skills to analyze information, evaluate evidence, and formulate reasoned arguments. This involves synthesizing information from multiple sources, identifying patterns or trends, and drawing logical conclusions.

8. Research and Source Integration : Conducting research and integrating sources effectively to support arguments or provide evidence. This includes evaluating sources for credibility and reliability, citing sources accurately, and avoiding plagiarism through proper attribution and citation.

9. Creativity and Originality : Expressing creativity and originality in writing to engage readers and convey unique perspectives. This involves using imaginative language, employing literary devices such as metaphor or imagery, and incorporating personal voice or style into the writing.

10. Revision and Editing : Revising and editing writing to improve clarity, coherence, and effectiveness. This includes reviewing content for errors in grammar, punctuation, and spelling, as well as refining ideas, restructuring sentences, and polishing language for clarity and impact.

By developing strong writing skills, students can communicate their ideas effectively, demonstrate their understanding of complex concepts, and engage with various audiences in academic, professional, and personal contexts. Writing skills are essential for success in school, work, and life, empowering students to express themselves confidently and persuasively through the written word.

Ideas for Study Material/Resources:
Books: "On Writing Well" by William Zinsser, "The Elements of Style" by William Strunk Jr. and E.B. White, "Bird by Bird" by Anne Lamott.
Online Courses: Platforms like Coursera, MasterClass, and Skillshare offer courses on writing skills, creative writing, and business writing, often taught by experienced authors and communication experts.
Articles and Blogs: Writing blogs, grammar websites, and literature magazines often feature articles on writing techniques, grammar rules, and style guides.

Ideas for Activity:
Conduct writing workshops where participants practice different writing styles and formats, such as persuasive writing, storytelling, and professional correspondence.
Assign writing assignments or prompts that challenge participants to apply specific writing techniques or communicate ideas effectively within constraints.

Some Training Ideas for Facilitation:
Start by defining writing skills and their importance in personal and professional communication.
Teach writing fundamentals, including grammar rules, sentence structure, and style guidelines, along with strategies for organizing ideas and revising drafts.
Provide opportunities for participants to practice writing in various genres and contexts, receive feedback, and refine their writing skills through constructive critique and revision.

Did You Know?
Strong writing skills are associated with higher academic achievement, better job performance, and increased earning potential across industries and occupations.

Ideas for Presentation:
Create a PowerPoint presentation or e-book summarizing key writing concepts, techniques, and best practices. Include examples, writing exercises, and before-and-after samples to illustrate the impact of effective writing.

Training Video Guide:
Develop video tutorials demonstrating specific writing techniques, such as crafting compelling introductions, using descriptive language, and structuring paragraphs.

Provide examples and analysis to help learners understand how to apply these techniques in their own writing.

Skill 38: Remote Work Skills

Importance:
Remote work skills are essential for effectively collaborating, communicating, and staying productive in a remote or distributed work environment. They encompass technical proficiency, self-discipline, and adaptability to remote tools and workflows.

Concept:
Remote work skills include proficiency in using remote collaboration tools (e.g., video conferencing, project management platforms), managing time effectively, maintaining work-life balance, and communicating clearly and proactively with remote team members.

Takeaway: Guide for Students and Professionals
By mastering remote work skills, individuals can thrive in virtual work settings, contribute effectively to remote teams, and achieve work objectives despite physical distance or time zone differences. Remote work skills are increasingly valuable in today's globalized and digitally connected workplace.
Remote work skills encompass a wide range of abilities that enable individuals to effectively collaborate, communicate, and manage tasks while working from a distance. These skills are essential for navigating the challenges and opportunities of remote work, whether from home, a co-working space, or another location.

Key components of remote work skills include:

1. Digital Literacy : Proficiency in using digital tools and platforms for communication, collaboration, and task management. This includes familiarity with email, video conferencing software, project management tools, cloud storage platforms, and other digital productivity tools.

2. Communication Skills : Effective written and verbal communication skills are crucial for remote work, as most interactions occur through email, chat, video calls, or phone calls. Clear and concise communication helps ensure that messages are understood and tasks are completed efficiently.

3. Time Management : The ability to manage time effectively and prioritize tasks while working remotely. This involves setting clear goals and deadlines, creating a daily or weekly schedule, and avoiding distractions to stay focused and productive.

4. Self-Motivation and Discipline : Remote work requires a high degree of self-motivation and discipline to maintain productivity and meet deadlines without direct supervision. This includes setting goals, establishing routines, and holding oneself accountable for completing tasks on time.

5. Adaptability and Flexibility : Being adaptable and flexible in response to changing priorities, schedules, or work environments. Remote work often requires individuals to juggle multiple tasks or projects simultaneously and to adjust to shifting circumstances quickly.

6. Problem-Solving Skills : The ability to identify and resolve issues independently while working remotely. This includes troubleshooting technical problems, addressing communication challenges, and finding creative solutions to overcome obstacles.

7. Collaboration and Teamwork : Collaborating effectively with colleagues and team members who may be located in different time zones or regions. This involves sharing information, coordinating tasks, and fostering a sense of camaraderie and mutual support despite physical distance.

8. Remote Leadership Skills : For those in leadership roles, the ability to lead and motivate remote teams effectively. This includes providing clear direction, offering support and feedback, and fostering a positive and inclusive team culture.

9. Tech Savviness : Staying up-to-date with technological advancements and trends relevant to remote work. This includes familiarity with remote work tools, cybersecurity best practices, and digital collaboration platforms.

10. Virtual Assistant : Utilizing virtual assistant tools and technologies to automate repetitive tasks, manage calendars, schedule meetings, and streamline administrative processes. Virtual assistants enhance efficiency and productivity, allowing individuals to focus on higher-value work tasks.

11. Wellness and Work-Life Balance : Prioritizing self-care and maintaining a healthy work-life balance while working remotely. This involves setting boundaries between work and personal life, taking regular breaks, and practicing mindfulness or stress management techniques.

By developing strong remote work skills, individuals can thrive in remote work environments, maximize their productivity, and contribute effectively to remote teams and projects. These skills are essential for achieving success in today's increasingly digital and interconnected world.

Ideas for Study Material/Resources:
Books: "Remote: Office Not Required" by Jason Fried and David Heinemeier Hansson, "The Year Without Pants: WordPress.com and the Future of Work" by Scott Berkun, "Digital Nomad" by Tsugio Makimoto and David Manners.
Online Courses: Platforms like LinkedIn Learning, Udemy, and Remote.co offer courses on remote work skills, virtual collaboration, and telecommuting best practices.
Articles and Blogs: Remote work blogs, productivity websites, and HR publications often feature articles on remote work strategies, remote team management, and remote work tools.

Ideas for Activity:
Conduct remote work simulation exercises where participants collaborate on virtual projects using remote collaboration tools and communication platforms.
Facilitate discussions or workshops on remote work best practices, challenges, and strategies for maintaining productivity and well-being in a remote work environment.

Some Training Ideas for Facilitation:
Start by defining remote work skills and their importance in the context of remote work trends and practices.
Teach technical skills for using remote collaboration tools, managing virtual meetings, and coordinating tasks and projects across distributed teams.
Provide guidance on time management, self-motivation, and maintaining work-life balance while working remotely, along with strategies for overcoming common challenges and distractions.

Did You Know?
Remote work is on the rise, with more companies adopting remote or hybrid work models to attract top talent, reduce overhead costs, and promote work-life balance.

Ideas for Presentation:
Create a PowerPoint presentation or e-book summarizing key remote work concepts, tools, and best practices. Include tips, case studies, and remote work success stories to inspire and inform remote workers and managers.

Training Video Guide:
Develop video tutorials demonstrating how to use remote collaboration tools effectively, manage virtual meetings, and maintain productivity while working remotely. Provide practical tips and real-life examples to help remote workers navigate the challenges of remote work and maximize their effectiveness in virtual work settings.

Skill 39: Social Media Management

Importance:
Social media management skills are crucial for businesses and individuals to effectively build and maintain an online presence, engage with audiences, and achieve marketing objectives. They involve strategies for content creation, community management, and social media analytics.

Concept:
Social media management encompasses the planning, execution, and monitoring of social media activities across various platforms, such as Facebook, Twitter, Instagram, LinkedIn, and YouTube. It involves creating and curating content, interacting with followers, and analyzing performance metrics to optimize social media efforts.

Takeaway: Guide for Students and Professionals

By mastering social media management skills, individuals and organizations can increase brand awareness, drive website traffic, generate leads, and foster customer relationships. Social media has become a powerful marketing and communication channel, offering opportunities for brand building and audience engagement.

Social media management skills are essential for individuals and businesses seeking to build and maintain a strong online presence, engage with audiences, and achieve their marketing and communication objectives across various social media platforms. These skills encompass a range of tasks related to content creation, scheduling, monitoring, analysis, and community management.

Key components of social media management skills include:

1. Platform Familiarity : Proficiency in using different social media platforms such as Facebook, Instagram, Twitter, LinkedIn, YouTube, Pinterest, and TikTok. Understanding the unique features, audience demographics, and best practices for each platform is essential for effective management.

2. Content Creation : Developing engaging and relevant content tailored to the target audience and platform. This includes creating text posts, images, videos, infographics, and other multimedia content that aligns with brand identity and communication goals.

3. Content Calendar Management : Planning and scheduling content in advance using content calendar tools or social media management platforms. This involves organizing content by date, time, and platform, as well as coordinating campaigns and promotions across multiple channels.

4. Audience Engagement : Actively engaging with followers, responding to comments, messages, and mentions, and fostering conversations to build relationships and strengthen brand loyalty. This includes acknowledging feedback, addressing customer inquiries, and resolving issues promptly and professionally.

5. Community Management : Cultivating and managing online communities by moderating discussions, facilitating user-generated content, and fostering a positive and inclusive environment. This involves enforcing community guidelines, monitoring user behavior, and addressing inappropriate or disruptive activity.

6. Analytics and Insights : Monitoring social media performance metrics such as engagement, reach, impressions, clicks, and conversions. Analyzing data and insights to evaluate the effectiveness of social media strategies, identify trends, and make informed decisions for optimization and improvement.

7. Paid Advertising : Understanding the fundamentals of social media advertising and leveraging paid promotional tools to reach target audiences, amplify content, and drive conversions. This includes setting campaign objectives, targeting specific demographics, and optimizing ad creative and budget allocation.

8. Trend Awareness : Staying informed about current trends, topics, and conversations relevant to the industry, audience interests, and social media landscape. Being able to leverage trends effectively can help increase visibility, relevance, and engagement on social media platforms.

9. Brand Management : Maintaining brand consistency and integrity across all social media channels. This involves adhering to brand guidelines, tone of voice, and visual identity standards, as well as representing the brand positively and authentically in all interactions.

10. Continuous Learning and Adaptation : Staying updated with the latest social media trends, algorithms, features, and best practices through ongoing learning and professional development. Being adaptable and flexible to evolving trends and changes in the social media landscape is essential for long-term success.

By developing strong social media management skills, individuals and businesses can effectively leverage social media platforms to connect with audiences, drive engagement, and achieve their marketing and communication objectives. These skills are valuable for building brand awareness, fostering customer relationships, and driving business growth in today's digital age.

Ideas for Study Material/Resources:
Books: "Jab, Jab, Jab, Right Hook: How to Tell Your Story in a Noisy Social World" by Gary Vaynerchuk, "Crushing It!: How Great Entrepreneurs Build Their Business and Influence—and How You Can, Too" by Gary Vaynerchuk, "500 Social Media Marketing Tips" by Andrew Macarthy.
Online Courses: Platforms like Udemy, Coursera, and HubSpot Academy offer courses on social media marketing, social media management tools, and content strategy.
Articles and Blogs: Social media blogs, marketing websites, and industry publications often feature articles on social media trends, best practices, and case studies.

Ideas for Activity:
Conduct social media strategy workshops where participants develop social media content calendars, define target audiences, and plan engagement tactics for different platforms.
Assign social media management projects or campaigns where participants apply social media management techniques to promote a product, service, or cause and track performance metrics.

Some Training Ideas for Facilitation:
Start by introducing participants to the fundamentals of social media management, including platform selection, audience targeting, and content strategy.
Teach social media best practices, such as creating engaging content, optimizing posts for each platform, and fostering meaningful interactions with followers.
Provide guidance on using social media management tools, scheduling posts, analyzing metrics, and adjusting strategies based on performance insights.

Did You Know?
Social media users spend an average of 2 hours and 24 minutes per day on social networking and messaging platforms, making social media a valuable channel for reaching and engaging with target audiences.

Ideas for Presentation:
Create a PowerPoint presentation or e-book summarizing key social media management concepts, strategies, and tools. Include examples, case studies, and actionable tips for building a successful social media presence.

Training Video Guide:
Develop video tutorials demonstrating how to create and optimize social media profiles, schedule and publish posts, engage with followers, and analyze social media metrics. Provide step-by-step instructions and real-life examples to help learners navigate the complexities of social media management effectively.

Skill 40: SEO (Search Engine Optimization)

Importance:
Search engine optimization (SEO) skills are essential for improving a website's visibility and ranking in search engine results pages (SERPs). They involve techniques for optimizing website content, building backlinks, and improving site performance to attract organic traffic.

Concept:
SEO encompasses strategies and tactics to increase a website's visibility in search engine results for relevant queries. It includes on-page optimization (e.g., keyword research, content optimization) and off-page optimization (e.g., link building, social media promotion) techniques to improve search engine rankings and drive organic traffic.

Takeaway: Guide for Students and Professionals
By mastering SEO skills, individuals and businesses can enhance their online presence, attract more targeted traffic, and achieve their marketing objectives. SEO is a cost-effective way to increase website visibility, generate leads, and grow online authority and credibility.

Search Engine Optimization (SEO) skills are essential for individuals and businesses seeking to improve their online visibility, drive organic traffic to their websites, and increase their rankings in search engine results pages (SERPs). SEO involves optimizing website content, structure, and performance to align with search engine algorithms and user intent, ultimately improving the website's chances of being discovered by potential customers or users.

Key components of SEO skills include:

1. Keyword Research : Conducting keyword research to identify relevant search terms and phrases that potential users or customers are using to find information related to

the website's content or products. This involves using keyword research tools to analyze search volume, competition, and keyword variations.

2. On-Page Optimization : Optimizing on-page elements such as titles, meta descriptions, headings, and body content to include target keywords and improve relevance to search queries. This also includes optimizing URL structures, internal linking, and image alt attributes for better indexing and ranking.

3. Content Creation and Optimization : Creating high-quality, relevant, and valuable content that addresses user needs and interests while incorporating target keywords naturally. This includes optimizing content for readability, relevance, and engagement, as well as updating and refreshing content regularly to maintain relevance.

4. Technical SEO : Ensuring that the website's technical infrastructure is optimized for search engine crawling and indexing. This involves addressing issues such as site speed, mobile-friendliness, crawlability, indexing directives, XML sitemaps, and schema markup to improve overall site performance and user experience.

5. Link Building : Building quality backlinks from authoritative and relevant websites to improve the website's authority and credibility in the eyes of search engines. This includes strategies such as guest blogging, content outreach, influencer collaborations, and social media promotion to earn natural, high-quality backlinks.

6. Local SEO : Optimizing the website for local search queries to improve visibility in local search results and attract customers from specific geographic areas. This includes optimizing Google My Business listings, local citations, and geo-targeted content, as well as encouraging customer reviews and ratings.

7. Analytics and Performance Monitoring : Monitoring website performance and SEO metrics using analytics tools such as Google Analytics and Google Search Console. This involves tracking key performance indicators (KPIs) such as organic traffic, keyword rankings, click-through rates (CTRs), and conversion rates to measure the effectiveness of SEO efforts.

8. User Experience (UX) Optimization : Improving the overall user experience of the website to enhance engagement, reduce bounce rates, and increase dwell time. This includes optimizing site navigation, page load times, mobile responsiveness, and overall usability to provide a seamless and satisfying experience for visitors.

9. Algorithm Updates and Trends : Staying informed about changes to search engine algorithms and industry trends to adapt SEO strategies accordingly. This involves keeping up-to-date with algorithm updates from major search engines such as Google, Bing, and Yahoo, as well as industry news and best practices.

10. Ethical and White-Hat Practices : Following ethical and white-hat SEO practices to comply with search engine guidelines and avoid penalties or sanctions. This includes avoiding black-hat tactics such as keyword stuffing, cloaking, link spamming, and other manipulative techniques that can harm the website's reputation and rankings.

By developing strong SEO skills, individuals and businesses can improve their online visibility, attract more organic traffic, and achieve their marketing and business objectives in today's competitive digital landscape. SEO skills are essential for driving sustainable growth, increasing brand awareness, and establishing authority and credibility in the online marketplace.

Ideas for Study Material/Resources:
Books: "SEO 2022: Learn Search Engine Optimization with Smart Internet Marketing Strategies" by Adam Clarke, "The Art of SEO" by Eric Enge, Stephan Spencer, Jessie Stricchiola, and Rand Fishkin, "SEO for Growth" by John Jantsch and Phil Singleton.
Online Courses: Platforms like Moz Academy, SEMrush Academy, and HubSpot Academy offer courses on SEO fundamentals, advanced SEO techniques, and SEO tools.
Articles and Blogs: SEO blogs, digital marketing websites, and search engine news platforms often feature articles on SEO trends, algorithm updates, and optimization strategies.

Ideas for Activity:
Conduct keyword research workshops where participants identify relevant keywords for their target audience and develop content optimization strategies based on keyword insights.
Organize SEO audits or website optimization projects where participants analyze website performance, identify optimization opportunities, and implement SEO best practices to improve search engine rankings.

Some Training Ideas for Facilitation:
Start by explaining the importance of SEO and its role in driving organic traffic and improving website visibility.
Teach fundamental SEO concepts, such as keyword research, on-page optimization, technical SEO, and link building strategies.
Provide practical guidance on using SEO tools, monitoring website performance, and measuring SEO success through key performance indicators (KPIs) such as organic traffic, keyword rankings, and backlink profiles.

Did You Know?
Websites that appear on the first page of Google search results receive approximately 95% of clicks, highlighting the importance of optimizing for search engines to attract organic traffic.

Ideas for Presentation:
Create a PowerPoint presentation or e-book summarizing key SEO concepts, strategies, and best practices. Include case studies, examples, and actionable tips for improving website visibility and search engine rankings.

Training Video Guide:
Develop video tutorials demonstrating how to perform SEO tasks such as conducting keyword research, optimizing website content, and building backlinks. Provide step-

by-step instructions, screen recordings, and real-life examples to help learners understand and apply SEO techniques effectively.

Skill 41: Content Creation and Management

Importance:
Content creation and management skills are essential for developing compelling and engaging content across various platforms, including websites, blogs, social media, and marketing materials. They involve crafting valuable and relevant content that resonates with the target audience and drives desired outcomes.

Concept:
Content creation and management encompass the planning, creation, publishing, and optimization of content to attract, engage, and retain audiences. It includes content strategy development, content ideation, content production, and content distribution techniques to achieve marketing goals and enhance brand visibility.

Takeaway: Guide for Students and Professionals
By mastering content creation and management skills, individuals and organizations can effectively communicate their message, establish thought leadership, and build relationships with their audience. Content is a cornerstone of digital marketing and plays a vital role in driving brand awareness, generating leads, and nurturing customer relationships.
Content creation and management skills are essential for individuals and businesses aiming to produce high-quality, engaging content across various platforms and channels to attract and retain audiences, drive engagement, and achieve their marketing and communication goals.

Key components of content creation and management skills include:

1. Content Strategy Development : Creating a comprehensive content strategy aligned with business objectives, target audience interests, and marketing goals. This involves defining content themes, topics, formats, and distribution channels, as well as establishing key performance indicators (KPIs) to measure success.

2. Audience Research and Persona Development : Conducting audience research to understand the needs, preferences, and behaviors of target audience segments. Developing buyer personas to represent different audience demographics and tailoring content to address their specific interests, pain points, and aspirations.

3. Content Ideation and Planning : Generating creative and relevant content ideas that resonate with target audiences and align with the brand's messaging and values. Planning content calendars and editorial schedules to ensure consistent publishing and distribution of content across channels.

4. Content Creation and Production : Generating various types of content, including articles, blog posts, videos, infographics, podcasts, social media posts, and interactive content. This involves writing, designing, recording, and editing content using appropriate tools and software, as well as adhering to brand guidelines and quality standards.

5. Search Engine Optimization (SEO) : Optimizing content for search engines to improve visibility, rankings, and organic traffic. This includes conducting keyword research, optimizing on-page elements, creating valuable and relevant content, and earning backlinks from authoritative sources.

6. Content Distribution and Promotion : Developing distribution strategies to reach target audiences through owned, earned, and paid channels. Promoting content through social media, email marketing, influencer partnerships, content syndication, and other promotional tactics to increase reach and engagement.

7. Community Engagement and Management : Engaging with audiences, fostering conversations, and building relationships through comments, shares, and interactions on social media, forums, and community platforms. Responding to feedback, addressing inquiries, and moderating discussions to maintain a positive and engaged community.

8. Analytics and Performance Monitoring : Tracking and analyzing content performance metrics to evaluate the effectiveness of content strategies and campaigns. Monitoring key metrics such as website traffic, engagement, conversion rates, and social media metrics to identify trends, opportunities, and areas for improvement.

9. Content Optimization and Iteration : Iterating and optimizing content based on performance data, audience feedback, and industry trends. Continuously refining content strategies, messaging, and formats to improve relevance, engagement, and conversion rates over time.

10. Content Governance and Compliance : Establishing content governance policies and processes to ensure consistency, quality, and compliance with legal and regulatory requirements. Implementing editorial guidelines, approval workflows, and content management systems (CMS) to manage content effectively and mitigate risks.

By developing strong content creation and management skills, individuals and businesses can create compelling, relevant, and valuable content that resonates with target audiences, drives engagement, and achieves marketing and business objectives. These skills are essential for building brand awareness, fostering customer relationships, and driving growth in today's competitive digital landscape.

Ideas for Study Material/Resources:
Books: "Content Rules: How to Create Killer Blogs, Podcasts, Videos, Ebooks, Webinars (and More) That Engage Customers and Ignite Your Business" by Ann Handley and C.C.

Chapman, "Everybody Writes: Your Go-To Guide to Creating Ridiculously Good Content" by Ann Handley.

Online Courses: Platforms like Coursera, HubSpot Academy, and Copyblogger offer courses on content marketing, content strategy, and content creation.

Articles and Blogs: Content marketing blogs, copywriting websites, and digital marketing publications often feature articles on content creation best practices, storytelling techniques, and content marketing trends.

Ideas for Activity:
Conduct content brainstorming sessions or workshops where participants generate content ideas, develop content calendars, and plan content campaigns aligned with business objectives.

Assign content creation projects or challenges where participants create various types of content, such as blog posts, videos, infographics, or social media posts, and track performance metrics to evaluate effectiveness.

Some Training Ideas for Facilitation:
Start by defining content creation and management and their importance in digital marketing and brand building.

Teach content strategy fundamentals, including audience research, content planning, content formats, and distribution channels.

Provide practical guidance on content creation techniques, such as storytelling, copywriting, visual design, and multimedia production, tailored to different platforms and audience preferences.

Did You Know?
Content marketing generates three times as many leads as traditional outbound marketing, highlighting the effectiveness of content in attracting and engaging audiences.

Ideas for Presentation:
Create a PowerPoint presentation or e-book summarizing key content creation and management concepts, strategies, and best practices. Include templates, checklists, and examples to help learners develop effective content marketing strategies and campaigns.

Training Video Guide:
Develop video tutorials demonstrating how to create various types of content, such as blog posts, videos, podcasts, and social media posts. Provide tips, examples, and best practices for crafting compelling content that resonates with the target audience and achieves marketing objectives.

Skill 42: Graphic Design Skills

Importance:
Graphic design skills are essential for creating visually appealing and effective designs across various mediums, including print and digital media. They involve understanding

design principles, using design software, and applying creativity to communicate messages visually.

Concept:
Graphic design skills encompass the ability to create visual content, such as logos, illustrations, infographics, and web graphics, that effectively communicates a message or idea. They involve knowledge of design principles, typography, color theory, and layout techniques to create aesthetically pleasing and impactful designs.

Takeaway: Guide for Students and Professionals
By mastering graphic design skills, individuals can create professional-looking designs, enhance brand identity, and convey complex information in a visually engaging manner. Graphic design is essential in various fields, including marketing, advertising, web design, and publishing, and can contribute to career advancement and creative expression.

Graphic design skills are essential for individuals and businesses involved in creating visual content for various purposes, including branding, marketing, communication, and user experience enhancement. These skills enable designers to effectively communicate ideas, convey messages, and evoke emotions through visual elements such as typography, imagery, color, and layout.

Key components of graphic design skills include:

1. Visual Communication : Understanding the principles of visual communication and design, including hierarchy, balance, contrast, alignment, and proximity. Applying these principles to create visually appealing and effective designs that communicate messages clearly and cohesively.

2. Typography : Selecting appropriate typefaces, fonts, and typography styles to convey tone, personality, and hierarchy in design compositions. Understanding typographic principles such as readability, legibility, kerning, leading, and tracking to enhance the visual impact and clarity of text.

3. Color Theory : Understanding the psychology and symbolism of color and applying color theory principles to create harmonious and effective color palettes. Considering factors such as color contrast, saturation, temperature, and cultural associations to evoke specific emotions and convey brand identity.

4. Image Editing and Manipulation : Proficiency in using graphic design software such as Adobe Photoshop, Illustrator, or Sketch to edit and manipulate images, photos, and illustrations. This includes techniques such as cropping, retouching, compositing, masking, and applying filters or effects to enhance visual appeal and relevance.

5. Layout and Composition : Designing layout compositions that effectively organize visual elements such as text, images, and graphics to create balance, hierarchy, and visual flow. Considering factors such as grid systems, whitespace, alignment, and proximity to optimize readability and usability.

6. Brand Identity Design : Creating cohesive and memorable brand identities, including logos, brand marks, icons, and visual assets that reflect the brand's personality, values, and positioning. Ensuring consistency in brand identity elements across various touchpoints and applications.

7. User Interface (UI) Design : Designing user interfaces for websites, mobile apps, and digital platforms that are intuitive, user-friendly, and visually engaging. Considering user experience principles, usability guidelines, and interaction patterns to create effective UI designs that meet user needs and goals.

8. Print Design : Designing collateral materials for print, such as brochures, flyers, posters, business cards, and packaging. Understanding print production processes, color profiles, and file formats to ensure accurate and high-quality output in print media.

9. Vector Graphics and Illustration : Creating vector-based graphics and illustrations using tools such as Adobe Illustrator or Affinity Designer. Developing custom illustrations, icons, symbols, and vector artwork that enhance visual storytelling and reinforce brand messaging.

10. Responsive Design and Adaptability : Designing responsive and adaptable layouts that can scale and adjust to different screen sizes, devices, and resolutions. Ensuring consistency in design elements and user experience across desktop, tablet, and mobile platforms.

By developing strong graphic design skills, individuals can create visually compelling and impactful designs that effectively communicate messages, engage audiences, and achieve specific design objectives. These skills are valuable for designers, marketers, entrepreneurs, and professionals across various industries seeking to enhance their visual communication and branding efforts.

Ideas for Study Material/Resources:
Books: "The Non-Designer's Design Book" by Robin Williams, "Graphic Design School: The Principles and Practice of Graphic Design" by David Dabner, Sandra Stewart, and Abbie Vickress, "Thinking with Type" by Ellen Lupton.
Online Courses: Platforms like Skillshare, LinkedIn Learning, and Adobe Creative Cloud offer courses on graphic design fundamentals, Adobe Illustrator, Photoshop, and InDesign.
Articles and Blogs: Graphic design blogs, design websites, and creative publications often feature articles on design inspiration, tutorials, and industry trends.

Ideas for Activity:
Conduct design workshops or challenges where participants create designs for specific projects or scenarios, such as designing a logo, poster, or social media graphic.
Assign design projects where participants apply design principles and techniques to create visual assets for real-world applications, such as branding materials, marketing collateral, or website layouts.

Some Training Ideas for Facilitation:
Start by introducing participants to the principles of graphic design, including typography, color theory, composition, and visual hierarchy.
Teach essential design software skills, such as Adobe Illustrator, Photoshop, and InDesign, and provide hands-on practice exercises to familiarize participants with design tools and techniques.
Offer guidance on design best practices, such as choosing appropriate fonts, using color effectively, creating balanced compositions, and optimizing designs for different mediums and devices.

Did You Know?
Studies have shown that visual content is more engaging and memorable than text alone, making graphic design skills valuable for capturing and retaining audience attention.

Ideas for Presentation:
Create a PowerPoint presentation or e-book summarizing key graphic design concepts, principles, and techniques. Include design examples, case studies, and practical tips for creating visually compelling designs.

Training Video Guide:
Develop video tutorials demonstrating how to use graphic design software and apply design principles to create various types of designs, such as logos, posters, and social media graphics. Provide step-by-step instructions, design tips, and real-world examples to help learners improve their graphic design skills.

Skill 43: Video Editing Skills

Importance:
Video editing skills are essential for creating polished and engaging video content for various purposes, including marketing, education, entertainment, and communication. They involve techniques for assembling, trimming, and enhancing video footage to convey a message effectively.

Concept:
Video editing skills encompass the ability to edit raw video footage into a cohesive and visually appealing final product. They include knowledge of video editing software, such as Adobe Premiere Pro, Final Cut Pro, or DaVinci Resolve, as well as techniques for cutting, transitions, effects, and audio editing.

Takeaway: Guide for Students and Professionals
By mastering video editing skills, individuals can create professional-quality videos that captivate audiences, convey messages effectively, and achieve desired outcomes. Video editing is a valuable skill in today's digital age, where video content plays a significant role in marketing, storytelling, and communication.

Video editing skills are essential for individuals and professionals involved in creating and producing video content for various purposes, including entertainment, marketing, education, and communication. These skills enable editors to transform raw footage into polished and engaging videos by manipulating visual and audio elements, enhancing storytelling, and achieving desired effects.

Key components of video editing skills include:

1. Familiarity with Video Editing Software : Proficiency in using video editing software such as Adobe Premiere Pro, Final Cut Pro, DaVinci Resolve, or Sony Vegas. Understanding the interface, tools, and features of the software is essential for efficient editing and post-production workflows.

2. Video Footage Organization : Organizing and managing video footage, audio files, and other media assets in a structured and accessible manner. This includes labeling, categorizing, and archiving media files to streamline the editing process and improve efficiency.

3. Editing Techniques : Mastering basic and advanced editing techniques to assemble video clips, trim, cut, and splice footage, and create seamless transitions between scenes. This involves understanding pacing, rhythm, and continuity to maintain visual flow and narrative coherence.

4. Color Correction and Grading : Adjusting and enhancing the color and visual appearance of video footage using color correction and grading techniques. This includes correcting exposure, white balance, contrast, and saturation, as well as applying creative color grading to achieve specific looks and moods.

5. Audio Editing and Mixing : Editing and mixing audio tracks, dialogue, music, and sound effects to enhance the overall audio quality and narrative impact of the video. This involves adjusting volume levels, removing background noise, adding effects, and synchronizing audio with video clips.

6. Visual Effects and Motion Graphics : Incorporating visual effects, motion graphics, titles, and animations to add visual interest and enhance storytelling. This includes creating and integrating graphics, text overlays, lower thirds, and visual effects such as transitions, overlays, and compositing.

7. Storyboarding and Storytelling : Planning and structuring video content using storyboards or shot lists to visualize the sequence of shots and scenes. Understanding narrative structure, pacing, and storytelling techniques to engage audiences and convey messages effectively.

8. Transitions and Effects : Using a variety of transitions and effects to create smooth and polished transitions between video clips and scenes. This includes fades, dissolves, wipes, zooms, and other transition effects to add visual interest and maintain viewer engagement.

9.   Rendering and Exporting : Rendering and exporting video projects in various formats and resolutions suitable for different distribution platforms and playback devices. Understanding video codecs, file formats, aspect ratios, and compression settings to optimize video quality and file size.

10.   Collaboration and Feedback : Collaborating with clients, colleagues, or stakeholders throughout the editing process and incorporating feedback to refine and improve video content. Communicating effectively, managing revisions, and delivering final video projects that meet client expectations and objectives.

By developing strong video editing skills, individuals can create compelling, professional-quality videos that captivate audiences, convey messages effectively, and achieve specific communication or marketing goals. These skills are valuable for video editors, filmmakers, content creators, marketers, educators, and professionals across various industries seeking to leverage the power of video for storytelling, engagement, and communication.

Ideas for Study Material/Resources:
Books: "In the Blink of an Eye: A Perspective on Film Editing" by Walter Murch, "The Filmmaker's Handbook" by Steven Ascher and Edward Pincus, "The Technique of Film and Video Editing: History, Theory, and Practice" by Ken Dancyger and Michael Rabiger.
Online Courses: Platforms like Udemy, LinkedIn Learning, and Skillshare offer courses on video editing fundamentals, advanced editing techniques, and specific editing software.
Articles and Blogs: Video editing blogs, filmmaking websites, and industry publications often feature articles on editing tips, software tutorials, and editing workflow best practices.

Ideas for Activity:
Conduct video editing workshops or challenges where participants edit raw footage into short videos based on specific themes or objectives.
Assign video editing projects where participants apply different editing techniques and styles to create videos for different purposes, such as promotional videos, educational videos, or vlogs.

Some Training Ideas for Facilitation:
Start by introducing participants to the basics of video editing, including editing terminology, editing software interface, and basic editing techniques.
Teach essential video editing skills, such as importing footage, trimming clips, adding transitions, applying effects, adjusting audio levels, and exporting final videos.
Provide guidance on advanced editing techniques, such as color correction, motion graphics, green screen compositing, and multi-camera editing, tailored to participants' skill levels and project requirements.

Did You Know?
The rise of online video platforms and social media has increased the demand for video content, making video editing skills highly sought after in various industries and professions.

Ideas for Presentation:
Create a PowerPoint presentation or e-book summarizing key video editing concepts, techniques, and best practices. Include video editing examples, before-and-after comparisons, and workflow diagrams to illustrate the video editing process.

Training Video Guide:
Develop video tutorials demonstrating how to perform common video editing tasks using popular editing software. Provide step-by-step instructions, keyboard shortcuts, and editing tips to help learners master video editing techniques and improve their editing efficiency.

Skill 44: Coding Skills (e.g., Python, Java)

Importance:
Coding skills are essential for individuals interested in software development, data analysis, automation, and problem-solving. They involve the ability to write, understand, and debug code in programming languages such as Python, Java, JavaScript, C++, and others.

Concept:
Coding skills encompass proficiency in programming languages and the ability to translate algorithms and logic into executable code. They involve understanding programming concepts, syntax, data structures, and algorithms to develop software applications, scripts, and algorithms.

Takeaway: Guide for Students and Professionals
By mastering coding skills, individuals can pursue careers in software development, data science, web development, and other technology-related fields. Coding skills enable individuals to create software solutions, automate tasks, analyze data, and solve complex problems efficiently.

Coding skills are essential for individuals pursuing careers in software development, data science, web development, and other fields that require programming expertise. Proficiency in coding enables individuals to create, modify, and debug software applications, analyze data, automate tasks, and solve complex problems using programming languages and frameworks.

Key components of coding skills include:

1. Programming Languages : Proficiency in one or more programming languages commonly used in software development and data analysis. Popular programming languages include:

- Python : A versatile and beginner-friendly language widely used for web development, data analysis, artificial intelligence, machine learning, scientific computing, and automation tasks.

- Java : A robust and widely adopted language known for its portability, scalability, and platform independence. Java is commonly used for building enterprise-level applications, web servers, Android mobile apps, and large-scale distributed systems.
- JavaScript : A versatile language used for client-side web development, including building interactive web applications, dynamic user interfaces, and browser-based games.
- C++ : A powerful and efficient language used for system programming, game development, high-performance computing, and building resource-intensive applications.
- C# : A modern and versatile language developed by Microsoft, commonly used for building Windows desktop applications, web applications, and games using the Unity game engine.
- R : A language and environment for statistical computing and data analysis, commonly used by data scientists, statisticians, and researchers for data visualization, modeling, and analysis.

2. Data Structures and Algorithms : Understanding fundamental data structures (e.g., arrays, linked lists, stacks, queues, trees, graphs) and algorithms (e.g., sorting, searching, recursion, dynamic programming) used to solve computational problems efficiently.

3. Problem-Solving Skills : Developing strong problem-solving skills to analyze problems, formulate algorithms, and implement solutions using programming languages and techniques. This involves breaking down complex problems into smaller, manageable tasks and applying logical reasoning and algorithmic thinking to solve them.

4. Software Development Principles : Understanding software development principles, methodologies, and best practices such as object-oriented programming (OOP), modular design, version control (e.g., Git), testing (e.g., unit testing, integration testing), and documentation.

5. Web Development Skills : Proficiency in web development technologies such as HTML, CSS, and JavaScript for building interactive and responsive websites, web applications, and user interfaces. Familiarity with web frameworks and libraries such as React, Angular, Vue.js, Django, and Flask is also beneficial.

6. Database Management : Understanding database concepts and query languages (e.g., SQL) for storing, retrieving, and manipulating data in relational databases (e.g., MySQL, PostgreSQL) or NoSQL databases (e.g., MongoDB, Firebase).

7. Version Control Systems : Proficiency in using version control systems such as Git for managing code repositories, tracking changes, collaborating with team members, and maintaining project history.

8. Debugging and Troubleshooting : Developing skills in debugging and troubleshooting code to identify and fix errors, exceptions, and performance issues

effectively. This involves using debugging tools, logging, and systematic approaches to isolate and resolve issues in code.

9. Documentation and Communication : Writing clear, concise, and well-documented code, comments, and documentation to explain the purpose, functionality, and usage of software components. Communicating effectively with team members, stakeholders, and users to gather requirements, provide updates, and solicit feedback.

10. Continuous Learning and Adaptation : Staying updated with new technologies, programming languages, frameworks, and industry trends through continuous learning, self-study, and participation in online courses, coding bootcamps, and community events. Being adaptable and flexible to learn and apply new skills as needed in evolving technology landscapes.

By developing strong coding skills, individuals can pursue rewarding careers in software development, data science, web development, and related fields, contributing to innovation, problem-solving, and technological advancement across various industries and domains.

Ideas for Study Material/Resources:
Books: "Python Crash Course" by Eric Matthes, "Java: A Beginner's Guide" by Herbert Schildt, "Automate the Boring Stuff with Python" by Al Sweigart.
Online Courses: Platforms like Codecademy, Udemy, and Coursera offer courses on programming languages, data science, web development, and software engineering.
Articles and Blogs: Coding blogs, programming websites, and developer communities often feature tutorials, coding challenges, and resources for learning programming languages.

Ideas for Activity:
Conduct coding workshops or coding challenges where participants solve programming problems, implement algorithms, or build small projects using the programming language of their choice.
Assign coding projects or assignments where participants develop software applications, scripts, or algorithms to solve real-world problems or automate repetitive tasks.

Some Training Ideas for Facilitation:
Start by introducing participants to the fundamentals of programming, including variables, data types, control structures, functions, and classes.
Teach programming language syntax, features, and best practices, focusing on the selected programming language(s) such as Python or Java.
Provide guidance on debugging techniques, code optimization, version control, and software development tools commonly used in the industry.

Did You Know?
Programming languages like Python and Java are among the most widely used languages in various industries, including software development, data science, web development, and automation.

Ideas for Presentation:
Create a PowerPoint presentation or e-book summarizing key programming concepts, syntax, and techniques for the selected programming language(s). Include code examples, diagrams, and exercises to reinforce learning and understanding.

Training Video Guide:
Develop video tutorials demonstrating coding concepts, programming exercises, and project walkthroughs using the selected programming language(s). Provide explanations, code demonstrations, and debugging tips to help learners grasp programming concepts effectively.

Skill 45: Data Visualization (Charts, Tableau)

Importance:
Data visualization skills are crucial for effectively communicating insights and trends from data to stakeholders. They involve transforming raw data into visually appealing and easy-to-understand charts, graphs, and dashboards using tools like Tableau, Excel, or Python libraries like Matplotlib and Seaborn.

Concept:
Data visualization skills encompass the ability to select appropriate visualization techniques, design visually compelling graphics, and interpret data trends and patterns. They involve understanding data types, visualization principles, and best practices for creating informative and engaging data visualizations.

Takeaway: Guide for Students and Professionals
By mastering data visualization skills, individuals can effectively convey complex data insights to diverse audiences, support decision-making processes, and drive data-driven strategies. Data visualization plays a crucial role in data analysis, reporting, and storytelling across various industries and domains.
Proficiency in Microsoft Excel is essential for individuals and professionals involved in data analysis, reporting, and visualization. Excel offers powerful features and functionalities for managing, analyzing, and visualizing data, making it a widely used tool in various industries and domains.

Key components of Excel skills for data visualization include:

1. Data Import and Cleaning : Importing data from external sources into Excel and cleaning it to remove duplicates, errors, and inconsistencies. This involves tasks such as data validation, text-to-columns, find and replace, and filtering to prepare the data for analysis and visualization.

2. Data Manipulation and Transformation : Performing data manipulation and transformation tasks in Excel to restructure, aggregate, and summarize data as needed for visualization. This includes using functions such as SUM, AVERAGE, COUNT, IF, VLOOKUP, and pivot tables to analyze and organize data effectively.

3. Chart Creation : Creating various types of charts and graphs in Excel to visualize data and highlight trends, patterns, and relationships. Excel offers a range of chart types including column charts, line charts, pie charts, bar charts, scatter plots, and histograms, which can be customized and formatted to suit specific visualization needs.

4. Conditional Formatting : Applying conditional formatting rules to highlight data points, trends, or outliers in Excel worksheets. This enables users to visually identify important insights and exceptions within the data, such as using color scales, data bars, and icon sets to represent different levels of values.

5. Sparklines : Using sparklines in Excel to create miniaturized charts within individual cells, providing a quick visual summary of data trends. Sparklines are useful for displaying trends over time or comparing data points within a small space, such as in tables or dashboards.

6. Data Visualization Techniques : Applying various data visualization techniques and best practices within Excel to create clear and effective visualizations. This includes choosing appropriate chart types, adjusting axes, labels, and titles, and ensuring visualizations are easy to interpret and understand.

7. Dashboard Creation : Building interactive dashboards and reports in Excel to present data visualizations and analysis in a structured and accessible format. Excel dashboards can include multiple charts, tables, slicers, and interactive elements to provide a comprehensive view of the data and enable exploration.

8. Chart Customization : Customizing chart elements such as colors, fonts, labels, legends, and axes in Excel to enhance visual appeal and clarity. Excel provides a range of customization options to tailor visualizations to specific preferences and branding requirements.

9. Data Analysis Tools : Using built-in data analysis tools and features in Excel, such as pivot tables, pivot charts, data tables, and what-if analysis tools, to perform advanced data analysis and scenario modeling. These tools enable users to gain deeper insights into their data and make informed decisions.

10. Sharing and Collaboration : Sharing Excel workbooks and visualizations with colleagues or stakeholders and collaborating on data analysis projects. Excel offers features for sharing workbooks via email, OneDrive, or SharePoint, as well as for protecting sensitive data and controlling access permissions.

By developing strong Excel skills for data visualization, individuals can effectively analyze, visualize, and communicate insights from their data, enabling better decision-making and driving business success. Excel skills are valuable for analysts, managers, researchers, educators, and professionals across industries seeking to leverage data for analysis, reporting, and decision support.

Ideas for Study Material/Resources:
Books: "The Visual Display of Quantitative Information" by Edward R. Tufte, "Storytelling with Data: A Data Visualization Guide for Business Professionals" by Cole Nussbaumer Knaflic, "Tableau Your Data!: Fast and Easy Visual Analysis with Tableau Software" by Dan Murray and Christian Chabot.
Online Courses: Platforms like Coursera, Udemy, and LinkedIn Learning offer courses on data visualization techniques, Tableau software, and data storytelling.
Articles and Blogs: Data visualization blogs, data science websites, and analytics publications often feature articles on visualization tools, techniques, and case studies.

Ideas for Activity:
Organize data visualization workshops or challenges where participants create visualizations from provided datasets or real-world data scenarios using tools like Tableau or Excel.
Assign data visualization projects where participants analyze data, design custom visualizations, and create interactive dashboards to present insights and findings.

Some Training Ideas for Facilitation:
Start by explaining the importance of data visualization in data analysis, reporting, and decision-making processes.
Teach data visualization principles, including chart selection, color theory, layout design, and storytelling techniques to effectively communicate insights.
Provide hands-on training on data visualization tools like Tableau, covering data connection, visualization creation, dashboard design, and interactive features.

Did You Know?
Data visualization allows individuals to uncover hidden patterns, trends, and relationships in data that may not be apparent from raw data alone, leading to better-informed decisions and actions.

Ideas for Presentation:
Create a PowerPoint presentation or e-book summarizing key data visualization concepts, techniques, and best practices. Include examples, case studies, and design tips to help learners create impactful data visualizations.

Training Video Guide:
Develop video tutorials demonstrating data visualization techniques, chart creation, and dashboard design using tools like Tableau or Excel. Provide step-by-step instructions, best practices, and real-world examples to help learners master data visualization skills.

Skill 46: Cybersecurity Awareness

Importance:
Cybersecurity awareness is crucial in today's digital age to protect personal and organizational data from cyber threats, such as malware, phishing attacks, and data

breaches. It involves understanding common cyber threats, implementing security best practices, and maintaining vigilance to safeguard digital assets.

Concept:
Cybersecurity awareness encompasses knowledge of potential cyber threats, vulnerabilities, and security measures to mitigate risks. It involves recognizing suspicious activities, practicing good cyber hygiene, and adhering to security policies and procedures to prevent unauthorized access and data compromise.

Takeaway: Guide for Students and Professionals
By mastering cybersecurity awareness, individuals can protect themselves and their organizations from cyber threats, minimize the risk of data breaches and financial losses, and maintain trust and confidence in digital interactions. Cybersecurity awareness is essential for both personal and professional cybersecurity hygiene.
Cybersecurity awareness is critical for individuals and organizations to protect sensitive information, safeguard digital assets, and mitigate cybersecurity risks. It involves understanding common cyber threats, adopting best practices for cybersecurity hygiene, and staying vigilant against emerging threats in the digital landscape.

Key components of cybersecurity awareness include:

1. Password Security : Utilize strong, unique passwords for each online account and enable multi-factor authentication (MFA) whenever possible.

2. Phishing Awareness : Exercise caution with suspicious emails, messages, or links, and verify the sender's identity before taking any action.

3. Social Media Safety : Limit the sharing of personal information on social media platforms and adjust privacy settings to control access to your content.

4. Software Updates : Keep software applications, operating systems, and antivirus programs up-to-date with the latest security patches and updates.

5. Safe Web Browsing : Avoid visiting suspicious websites or clicking on pop-up ads, and use browser security features to block malicious content.

6. Device Security : Secure devices with passwords, PINs, or biometric authentication, and install antivirus software to protect against unauthorized access.

7. Data Protection : Encrypt sensitive data and regularly back up important files to prevent data loss due to ransomware or hardware failure.

8. Wi-Fi Security : Connect to secure Wi-Fi networks with encryption when accessing the internet, especially in public places.

9. Incident Reporting : Report any suspicious activity or cybersecurity incidents to the appropriate authorities or IT support staff promptly.

10. Continuous Learning : Stay informed about cybersecurity threats and best practices through online resources and awareness training to safeguard yourself and others online.

Cybersecurity awareness is essential for students to stay safe and secure in an increasingly digital world. By implementing these practices, students can protect themselves from online threats and navigate the internet with confidence.

Ideas for Study Material/Resources:
Books: "Cybersecurity for Beginners" by Raef Meeuwisse, "The Art of Invisibility: The World's Most Famous Hacker Teaches You How to Be Safe in the Age of Big Brother and Big Data" by Kevin Mitnick, "The Cybersecurity Canon: Books Every Cybersecurity Professional Should Read" by Rick Howard.
Online Courses: Platforms like Cybrary, Udemy, and Coursera offer courses on cybersecurity fundamentals, ethical hacking, and security awareness training.
Articles and Blogs: Cybersecurity blogs, tech websites, and security publications often feature articles on cybersecurity threats, best practices, and industry trends.

Ideas for Activity:
Conduct cybersecurity awareness workshops or seminars where participants learn about common cyber threats, phishing simulations, and security best practices.
Organize cybersecurity awareness campaigns or challenges to raise awareness and promote good cyber hygiene practices among employees or community members.

Some Training Ideas for Facilitation:
Start by explaining the importance of cybersecurity awareness in protecting against cyber threats and maintaining digital security.
Teach participants about common cyber threats, such as malware, phishing, ransomware, and social engineering attacks, and how to recognize and respond to them.
Provide guidance on cybersecurity best practices, including password management, software updates, safe browsing habits, and data protection measures to secure personal and organizational assets.

Did You Know?
Cybersecurity incidents, such as data breaches and cyberattacks, can have significant financial and reputational consequences for individuals and organizations, highlighting the importance of cybersecurity awareness and preparedness.

Ideas for Presentation:
Create a PowerPoint presentation or e-book summarizing key cybersecurity awareness concepts, threats, and best practices. Include examples, case studies, and practical tips to help learners enhance their cybersecurity knowledge and protect against cyber threats.

Training Video Guide:
Develop video tutorials or security awareness videos highlighting common cyber threats, security tips, and best practices. Provide real-world examples, demonstrations, and scenarios to engage learners and reinforce cybersecurity awareness concepts.

Skill 47: Cloud Computing

Importance:
Cloud computing is a foundational technology that enables organizations and individuals to access and use computing resources over the internet on-demand. It offers scalability, flexibility, and cost-effectiveness, making it essential for digital transformation, innovation, and business agility.

Concept:
Cloud computing encompasses the delivery of computing services, including servers, storage, databases, networking, software, and analytics, over the internet. It involves understanding cloud deployment models (public, private, hybrid), service models (IaaS, PaaS, SaaS), and cloud architecture to leverage cloud resources effectively.

Takeaway: Guide for Students and Professionals
By mastering cloud computing, individuals can leverage cloud services to build, deploy, and manage applications, store and analyze data, and scale infrastructure dynamically. Cloud computing skills are essential for IT professionals, developers, and business leaders to drive digital innovation and competitive advantage.

Cloud computing is a transformative technology that offers individuals and organizations the ability to access computing resources and services over the internet on-demand, without the need for physical infrastructure or hardware. It enables users to store, manage, and process data, run applications, and scale resources dynamically, providing flexibility, scalability, and cost-efficiency.

Key components and concepts of cloud computing include:

1. Infrastructure as a Service (IaaS) : Provides virtualized computing infrastructure, including servers, storage, networking, and virtual machines (VMs), on a pay-as-you-go basis. Users can provision and manage resources dynamically to meet their specific requirements.

2. Platform as a Service (PaaS) : Offers a development and deployment platform with tools, libraries, and services for building, testing, and deploying applications without the need to manage underlying infrastructure. PaaS enables developers to focus on coding and innovation without worrying about hardware or software setup.

3. Software as a Service (SaaS) : Delivers software applications over the internet on a subscription basis, eliminating the need for installation, maintenance, and updates. Users can access SaaS applications through web browsers or APIs, enabling collaboration, productivity, and business process automation.

4. Public Cloud : Infrastructure and services provided by third-party cloud service providers (CSPs) and accessible to the general public over the internet. Public cloud offers scalability, cost-effectiveness, and convenience, with resources shared among multiple users and organizations.

5. Private Cloud : Dedicated cloud infrastructure and services operated and managed by a single organization or hosted by a third-party provider exclusively for that organization's use. Private cloud offers enhanced security, control, and customization compared to public cloud but requires higher upfront investment and operational overhead.

6. Hybrid Cloud : Integration of public and private cloud environments to enable workload portability, data sharing, and flexibility. Hybrid cloud allows organizations to leverage the scalability and cost-effectiveness of public cloud while maintaining sensitive data and critical workloads on-premises or in a private cloud.

7. Cloud Storage : Storage services offered by cloud providers for storing and accessing data over the internet. Cloud storage solutions provide scalability, durability, and accessibility, with options for object storage, file storage, and block storage tailored to different use cases and requirements.

8. Cloud Security : Implementation of security measures and best practices to protect data, applications, and infrastructure in the cloud. Cloud security encompasses identity and access management (IAM), encryption, network security, compliance, and threat detection and response to mitigate risks and ensure data confidentiality, integrity, and availability.

9. Serverless Computing : Cloud computing model where cloud providers manage the infrastructure and dynamically allocate resources to run applications, scaling automatically based on demand. Serverless computing eliminates the need for provisioning and managing servers, allowing developers to focus on writing code and achieving business objectives.

10. Cloud Migration : Process of moving applications, data, and workloads from on-premises environments to the cloud or between cloud providers. Cloud migration involves assessing existing infrastructure, planning migration strategies, and executing migrations to optimize performance, cost, and resilience in the cloud.

Cloud computing revolutionizes the way individuals and organizations consume, manage, and deliver IT resources and services, driving innovation, agility, and efficiency in the digital era. By leveraging cloud technologies, businesses can accelerate digital transformation, improve scalability and agility, and unlock new opportunities for growth and innovation.

Ideas for Study Material/Resources:
Books: "Cloud Computing: Concepts, Technology & Architecture" by Thomas Erl, "AWS Certified Solutions Architect Study Guide" by Ben Piper and David Clinton, "Microsoft Azure Essentials" by Michael Collier and Robin Shahan.
Online Courses: Platforms like AWS Training and Certification, Microsoft Learn, and Google Cloud Training offer courses on cloud computing fundamentals, cloud platforms, and certification preparation.
Articles and Blogs: Cloud computing blogs, vendor documentation, and tech publications often feature articles on cloud trends, best practices, and case studies.

Ideas for Activity:
Conduct cloud computing workshops or labs where participants gain hands-on experience with cloud platforms, services, and deployment scenarios.
Organize cloud computing hackathons or projects where participants build and deploy cloud-based solutions to solve real-world problems or innovate new products/services.

Some Training Ideas for Facilitation:
Start by introducing participants to the fundamentals of cloud computing, including key concepts, benefits, and use cases.
Teach participants about major cloud providers (AWS, Azure, Google Cloud), their core services, and how to choose the right cloud platform for specific use cases.
Provide guidance on cloud deployment, migration strategies, security best practices, cost management, and performance optimization to maximize the value of cloud computing investments.

Did You Know?
The global cloud computing market is projected to reach billions of dollars in revenue, indicating the increasing adoption and significance of cloud technologies across industries and sectors.

Ideas for Presentation:
Create a PowerPoint presentation or e-book summarizing key cloud computing concepts, deployment models, and best practices. Include diagrams, case studies, and practical examples to help learners understand and apply cloud computing principles effectively.

Training Video Guide:
Develop video tutorials or demonstrations illustrating cloud computing concepts, platform features, and deployment scenarios. Provide step-by-step instructions, tips, and troubleshooting techniques to help learners navigate cloud platforms and services confidently.

Skill 48: Database Management

Importance:
Database management is essential for organizing, storing, retrieving, and managing data efficiently and securely. It involves designing database schemas, optimizing performance, ensuring data integrity, and implementing backup and recovery strategies to support business operations and decision-making.

Concept:
Database management encompasses the design, implementation, maintenance, and optimization of databases to meet the data needs of organizations. It involves understanding database models (relational, NoSQL), database languages (SQL, NoSQL query languages), and database management systems (e.g., MySQL, PostgreSQL, MongoDB).

Takeaway: Guide for Students and Professionals
By mastering database management, individuals can design and maintain databases that support data-driven decision-making, business processes, and application development. Database management skills are essential for IT professionals, data analysts, developers, and business leaders across industries.

Database management involves the organization, storage, retrieval, and maintenance of data in a structured format, typically within a database system. It plays a crucial role in ensuring data integrity, security, and efficiency for organizations of all sizes across various industries.

Key components and concepts of database management include:

1. Relational Database Management Systems (RDBMS) : RDBMS is a software system that enables users to create, manage, and interact with relational databases. It organizes data into tables with rows and columns, enforces data integrity through constraints, and supports SQL (Structured Query Language) for querying and manipulating data.

2. Data Modeling : Data modeling involves designing the structure of a database to represent real-world entities, relationships, and constraints. It includes defining tables, columns, keys (e.g., primary keys, foreign keys), indexes, and relationships between tables to ensure data integrity and optimize query performance.

3. Database Design : Database design encompasses the process of creating and optimizing database schemas based on data modeling requirements. It involves normalization to reduce data redundancy and anomalies, denormalization for performance optimization, and choosing appropriate data types and constraints for efficient storage and retrieval.

4. Data Manipulation : Data manipulation involves inserting, updating, deleting, and querying data within a database using SQL statements or graphical user interfaces

(GUIs). Users can perform CRUD operations (Create, Read, Update, Delete) to manage data effectively and ensure consistency and accuracy.

5. Database Administration : Database administration includes tasks such as installation, configuration, monitoring, backup and recovery, security management, and performance tuning of database systems. Database administrators (DBAs) ensure the reliability, availability, and performance of databases to meet organizational needs and compliance requirements.

6. Data Security : Data security measures protect databases from unauthorized access, manipulation, or disclosure. It includes implementing access controls, encryption, authentication, and auditing mechanisms to enforce data privacy and compliance with regulations such as GDPR (General Data Protection Regulation) and HIPAA (Health Insurance Portability and Accountability Act).

7. Data Backup and Recovery : Database backup and recovery strategies involve creating regular backups of database contents and transaction logs to prevent data loss in case of system failures, disasters, or human errors. It includes implementing backup schedules, storage options, and recovery procedures to restore databases to a consistent state.

8. Scalability and Performance : Database scalability refers to the ability to handle increasing workloads and data volumes without sacrificing performance or availability. It involves horizontal scaling (adding more servers) or vertical scaling (upgrading server resources) to accommodate growth and optimize resource utilization.

9. Data Warehousing and Analytics : Data warehousing involves consolidating and integrating data from multiple sources into a centralized repository for analysis and reporting. It enables organizations to derive insights, make informed decisions, and improve business processes through data-driven decision-making.

10. Database Technologies : Various database technologies and models exist, including relational databases (e.g., MySQL, PostgreSQL, Oracle), NoSQL databases (e.g., MongoDB, Cassandra, Redis), NewSQL databases (e.g., CockroachDB, Google Spanner), and cloud-based database services (e.g., Amazon RDS, Azure SQL Database, Google Cloud SQL).

Effective database management is essential for organizations to leverage data as a strategic asset, drive innovation, and gain a competitive advantage in today's data-driven world. By implementing robust database management practices and leveraging appropriate technologies, organizations can ensure data integrity, security, and availability while maximizing the value of their data assets.

Ideas for Study Material/Resources:
Books: "Database Systems: The Complete Book" by Hector Garcia-Molina, Jennifer Widom, and Jeffrey D. Ullman, "SQL Performance Explained" by Markus Winand, "NoSQL Distilled: A Brief Guide to the Emerging World of Polyglot Persistence" by Pramod J. Sadalage and Martin Fowler.

Online Courses: Platforms like Udemy, Coursera, and Pluralsight offer courses on database management fundamentals, SQL, NoSQL databases, and database administration.

Articles and Blogs: Database management blogs, tech websites, and industry publications often feature articles on database trends, best practices, and case studies.

Ideas for Activity:

Conduct database management workshops or labs where participants learn database design principles, SQL query writing, and database administration tasks.

Organize database management projects where participants design and implement databases for specific use cases, such as e-commerce, inventory management, or customer relationship management.

Some Training Ideas for Facilitation:

Start by introducing participants to the fundamentals of database management, including database models, normalization, and database management systems (DBMS).

Teach participants SQL (Structured Query Language) for querying and manipulating relational databases, covering basic to advanced SQL concepts like joins, subqueries, and stored procedures.

Provide guidance on database administration tasks, such as backup and recovery, security management, performance tuning, and scalability planning, tailored to different database management systems and environments.

Did You Know?

Effective database management is critical for ensuring data consistency, reliability, and availability, which are essential for supporting business operations, analytics, and decision-making processes.

Ideas for Presentation:

Create a PowerPoint presentation or e-book summarizing key database management concepts, SQL queries, and best practices. Include database diagrams, SQL code examples, and troubleshooting tips to help learners understand and apply database management principles effectively.

Training Video Guide:

Develop video tutorials or demonstrations illustrating database management concepts, SQL query writing, and database administration tasks. Provide real-world examples, SQL query walkthroughs, and troubleshooting techniques to help learners develop practical database management skills.

Skill 49: UX/UI Design

Importance:

UX/UI (User Experience/User Interface) design is crucial for creating digital products and interfaces that are intuitive, user-friendly, and visually appealing. It involves understanding user needs, designing interactive prototypes, and optimizing the user journey to enhance usability and satisfaction.

Concept:
UX/UI design encompasses the process of understanding user behaviors, preferences, and goals to create effective digital experiences. It involves user research, wireframing, prototyping, visual design, and usability testing to create seamless and engaging user interfaces across websites, mobile apps, and software applications.

Takeaway: Guide for Students and Professionals
By mastering UX/UI design, individuals can create digital products and interfaces that delight users, drive engagement, and achieve business objectives. UX/UI design skills are essential for designers, developers, product managers, and business professionals involved in creating digital experiences.
UX/UI design, short for User Experience (UX) and User Interface (UI) design, focuses on creating intuitive, engaging, and visually appealing digital experiences for users across various devices and platforms. It encompasses understanding user needs, designing interfaces, and optimizing interactions to enhance user satisfaction and usability.

Key components and concepts of UX/UI design include:

1. User Research : User research involves gathering insights into user behaviors, preferences, and pain points through methods such as surveys, interviews, personas, and usability testing. It helps designers understand user needs and design solutions that meet those needs effectively.

2. Information Architecture : Information architecture (IA) defines the structure, organization, and navigation of content within digital products or websites. It includes creating sitemaps, user flows, and navigation systems to ensure users can find information and complete tasks efficiently.

3. Wireframing and Prototyping · Wireframing and prototyping are iterative design processes that involve creating low-fidelity sketches or interactive mockups to visualize and test design concepts. It helps designers validate ideas, gather feedback, and iterate on designs before final implementation.

4. Visual Design : Visual design focuses on the aesthetics and branding of digital interfaces, including layout, typography, color schemes, imagery, and iconography. It aims to create visually appealing designs that reinforce brand identity and engage users effectively.

5. Interaction Design : Interaction design (IxD) defines how users interact with digital interfaces and responds to their actions. It includes designing intuitive navigation, feedback mechanisms, animations, and micro-interactions to enhance user engagement and usability.

6. Responsive Design : Responsive design ensures digital interfaces adapt seamlessly to different screen sizes and devices, providing a consistent user experience across desktops, tablets, and smartphones. It involves using flexible layouts, fluid grids, and media queries to optimize content presentation and interaction on various devices.

7. Accessibility : Accessibility ensures digital products are usable by people of all abilities, including those with disabilities or impairments. It involves designing interfaces with considerations for accessibility standards (e.g., WCAG), providing alternative text for images, keyboard navigation, and screen reader compatibility.

8. Usability Testing : Usability testing involves observing users interacting with prototypes or live products to identify usability issues and gather feedback for improvement. It helps validate design decisions, prioritize enhancements, and optimize user experiences based on real-user insights.

9. Iterative Design Process : UX/UI design follows an iterative design process, where designers continuously gather feedback, iterate on designs, and refine solutions based on user insights and stakeholder input. It allows for flexibility and adaptation to evolving user needs and project requirements.

10. Collaboration and Communication : UX/UI design involves collaboration with cross-functional teams, including product managers, developers, marketers, and stakeholders. Effective communication and collaboration ensure alignment on project goals, user needs, and design solutions throughout the design process.

By integrating UX/UI design principles and methodologies into product development processes, organizations can create digital experiences that delight users, drive engagement, and achieve business objectives effectively. UX/UI design is a multifaceted discipline that encompasses both the user experience (UX) and user interface (UI) aspects of digital product design. It focuses on creating intuitive, visually appealing, and user-friendly experiences that meet the needs and preferences of the target audience. Whether designing websites, mobile apps, or software interfaces, UX/UI designers strive to optimize usability, accessibility, and overall user satisfaction through research, design, and iteration. From understanding user behaviors and preferences to crafting seamless interactions and visually appealing interfaces, UX/UI design plays a crucial role in shaping the success of digital products in today's competitive landscape.

Ideas for Study Material/Resources:
Books: "Don't Make Me Think" by Steve Krug, "The Design of Everyday Things" by Don Norman, "Sprint: How to Solve Big Problems and Test New Ideas in Just Five Days" by Jake Knapp, John Zeratsky, and Braden Kowitz.
Online Courses: Platforms like Udemy, Coursera, and Interaction Design Foundation offer courses on UX/UI design principles, tools, and techniques.
Articles and Blogs: UX/UI design blogs, design websites, and UX/UI communities often feature articles on design trends, best practices, and case studies.

Ideas for Activity:
Conduct UX/UI design workshops or design sprints where participants collaborate to solve design challenges, create wireframes, and prototype digital interfaces.
Organize design critiques or usability testing sessions where participants evaluate and provide feedback on each other's design prototypes or existing digital products.

Some Training Ideas for Facilitation:
Start by introducing participants to the principles of UX/UI design, including user-centered design, information architecture, and visual hierarchy.
Teach participants design tools and techniques for wireframing, prototyping, and visual design, such as Sketch, Adobe XD, Figma, or InVision.
Provide guidance on conducting user research, creating personas, designing user flows, and conducting usability testing to validate design decisions and iterate on designs effectively.

Did You Know?
A well-designed user interface can increase user satisfaction, reduce errors, and improve conversion rates, leading to better user engagement and business outcomes.

Ideas for Presentation:
Create a PowerPoint presentation or e-book summarizing key UX/UI design principles, processes, and best practices. Include design examples, case studies, and design exercises to help learners understand and apply UX/UI design concepts effectively.

Training Video Guide:
Develop video tutorials or design walkthroughs demonstrating UX/UI design processes, tools, and techniques. Provide step-by-step instructions, design tips, and real-world examples to help learners develop practical UX/UI design skills.

Skill 50: Web/App Development

Importance:
Web/App development is essential for creating websites, web applications, and mobile applications that provide valuable services, information, and experiences to users. It involves designing, coding, and deploying digital solutions using programming languages, frameworks, and development tools.

Concept:
Web/App development encompasses the process of building and maintaining digital solutions for various platforms, devices, and browsers. It involves frontend development (client-side), backend development (server-side), database integration, and deployment to deliver responsive, scalable, and secure web and mobile experiences.

Takeaway: Guide for Students and Professionals
By mastering web/app development, individuals can create interactive and functional digital solutions that meet user needs, drive engagement, and achieve business

objectives. Web/app development skills are essential for developers, designers, product managers, and entrepreneurs involved in building digital products and services.

Web and app development involves the creation of software applications for various platforms, including web browsers, mobile devices, and desktop computers. It encompasses a range of technologies, languages, and frameworks to build functional, responsive, and user-friendly digital experiences.

Key components and concepts of web/app development include:

1. Frontend Development : Frontend development focuses on the user interface (UI) and user experience (UX) aspects of web and app development. It involves coding HTML, CSS, and JavaScript to create interactive and visually appealing interfaces that users interact with directly.

2. Backend Development : Backend development handles the server-side logic and database interactions of web and app applications. It involves programming languages such as Python, Java, PHP, Ruby, and frameworks like Node.js, Django, Flask, and Ruby on Rails to build the server-side components that power web applications.

3. Full-Stack Development : Full-stack development combines both frontend and backend development skills to create end-to-end web applications. Full-stack developers have proficiency in both frontend and backend technologies, allowing them to work on all aspects of application development.

4. Mobile Development : Mobile development focuses on creating applications for mobile devices such as smartphones and tablets. It involves platforms such as iOS (using Swift or Objective-C) and Android (using Java or Kotlin), as well as cross-platform frameworks like React Native, Flutter, and Xamarin for building apps that run on multiple platforms.

5. Responsive Design : Responsive design ensures that web applications and websites adapt to different screen sizes and devices, providing a consistent user experience across desktops, tablets, and smartphones. It involves using flexible layouts, media queries, and responsive frameworks like Bootstrap and Foundation.

6. Progressive Web Apps (PWAs) : PWAs are web applications that leverage modern web technologies to deliver app-like experiences to users, including offline access, push notifications, and home screen installation. PWAs use service workers, web app manifests, and other APIs to enhance performance and usability.

7. API Development : API (Application Programming Interface) development involves creating interfaces that allow different software systems to communicate and interact with each other. It enables integration with third-party services, data exchange, and interoperability between web and app applications.

8. Database Management : Database management involves storing, retrieving, and managing data in a structured format within a database system. It includes relational

databases like MySQL, PostgreSQL, and SQL Server, as well as NoSQL databases like MongoDB and Firebase for storing and querying data efficiently.

9. Security : Security is a crucial aspect of web and app development, involving measures to protect against common threats such as cross-site scripting (XSS), SQL injection, cross-site request forgery (CSRF), and data breaches. It includes implementing authentication, authorization, encryption, and secure coding practices to mitigate risks and protect user data.

10. Deployment and DevOps : Deployment and DevOps practices involve automating the process of deploying, testing, and monitoring web and app applications to ensure reliability, scalability, and performance. It includes continuous integration (CI), continuous delivery (CD), containerization (e.g., Docker), and cloud platforms (e.g., AWS, Azure, Google Cloud) for efficient deployment and management of applications.

By mastering these key components and concepts of web/app development, developers can create robust, scalable, and user-friendly applications that meet the needs and expectations of users and businesses alike.

Ideas for Study Material/Resources:
Books: "Eloquent JavaScript" by Marijn Haverbeke, "Learning Web Design: A Beginner's Guide to HTML, CSS, JavaScript, and Web Graphics" by Jennifer Robbins, "The Pragmatic Programmer: Your Journey to Mastery" by Andrew Hunt and David Thomas.
Online Courses: Platforms like Udemy, Coursera, and freeCodeCamp offer courses on web development fundamentals, frontend frameworks (e.g., React, Angular), backend technologies (e.g., Node.js, Django), and mobile app development.
Articles and Blogs: Web development blogs, coding websites, and developer communities often feature tutorials, code snippets, and best practices for web/app development.

Ideas for Activity:
Conduct web/app development bootcamps or coding workshops where participants build web pages, web applications, or mobile apps from scratch using HTML, CSS, JavaScript, and relevant frameworks.
Organize coding challenges or hackathons where participants collaborate to develop innovative web/app projects within a limited timeframe, showcasing their development skills and creativity.

Some Training Ideas for Facilitation:
Start by introducing participants to the basics of web/app development, including HTML, CSS, JavaScript, and the principles of responsive design.
Teach participants frontend development skills, such as building user interfaces, handling user interactions, and styling web/app components using HTML, CSS, and JavaScript.
Provide guidance on backend development concepts, server-side programming, database integration, API development, and deployment strategies to create full-stack web applications and mobile apps.

Did You Know?
Web/app development skills are in high demand across industries, with job opportunities ranging from frontend and backend developers to full-stack developers, mobile app developers, and software engineers.

Ideas for Presentation:
Create a PowerPoint presentation or e-book summarizing key web/app development concepts, technologies, and best practices. Include code examples, project ideas, and resources for further learning to help learners dive deeper into web/app development.

Training Video Guide:
Develop video tutorials or coding screencasts demonstrating web/app development techniques, coding challenges, and project walkthroughs. Provide explanations, code demonstrations, and troubleshooting tips to help learners build their web/app development skills effectively.

Skill 51: Agile Methodologies

Importance:
Agile methodologies are essential for managing and delivering projects in a flexible, iterative, and collaborative manner. They promote adaptive planning, continuous improvement, and customer-centricity, enabling teams to respond quickly to change and deliver value efficiently.

Concept:
Agile methodologies encompass a set of principles and practices for iterative development, such as Scrum, Kanban, and Extreme Programming (XP). They emphasize teamwork, transparency, feedback, and delivering working software in short iterations (sprints) to meet evolving customer requirements.

Takeaway: Guide for Students and Professionals
By mastering agile methodologies, individuals can lead and participate in agile teams to deliver projects with greater speed, flexibility, and customer satisfaction. Agile skills are essential for project managers, team leaders, developers, and stakeholders involved in software development and project management.
Agile methodologies are iterative and incremental approaches to software development that prioritize flexibility, collaboration, and continuous improvement. They emphasize delivering value to customers through early and frequent releases, adapting to changing requirements, and fostering a culture of collaboration and accountability among cross-functional teams.

Key components and concepts of agile methodologies include:

1. Iterative Development : Agile development follows an iterative approach, where software is developed incrementally in small, manageable increments called iterations

or sprints. Each iteration typically lasts two to four weeks and results in a potentially shippable product increment.

2. Scrum Framework : Scrum is one of the most popular agile frameworks, emphasizing collaboration, transparency, and adaptability. It includes roles such as Scrum Master, Product Owner, and Development Team, as well as ceremonies like Sprint Planning, Daily Standups, Sprint Review, and Sprint Retrospective.

3. Kanban Method : Kanban is another agile framework that focuses on visualizing work, limiting work in progress (WIP), and optimizing workflow efficiency. It uses Kanban boards to visualize tasks and workflow stages, with a focus on continuous delivery and flow-based progress.

4. Cross-Functional Teams : Agile teams are cross-functional, consisting of members with diverse skills and expertise needed to deliver a complete product increment. Cross-functional teams collaborate closely to define, build, test, and deliver features, fostering a sense of ownership and shared responsibility.

5. User Stories : User stories are concise, user-centric descriptions of desired functionality from the perspective of end-users or stakeholders. They serve as the basis for prioritizing and planning work, focusing on delivering value to customers and addressing their needs effectively.

6. Product Backlog : The product backlog is a prioritized list of features, enhancements, and fixes that need to be implemented in the product. It is managed by the Product Owner and serves as a dynamic repository of requirements and ideas for the development team to work on.

7. Sprint Planning : Sprint planning is a collaborative meeting where the development team selects items from the product backlog to work on during the upcoming sprint. It involves defining sprint goals, breaking down user stories into tasks, estimating effort, and committing to deliverables for the sprint.

8. Daily Standups : Daily standups, also known as daily scrums, are brief, time boxed meetings where team members synchronize their activities, discuss progress, and identify any impediments. It fosters communication, alignment, and transparency among team members.

9. Sprint Review : Sprint review is a meeting held at the end of each sprint to demonstrate the completed work to stakeholders and gather feedback. It provides an opportunity to validate assumptions, collect input, and make course corrections based on stakeholder feedback.

10. Sprint Retrospective : Sprint retrospective is a meeting held at the end of each sprint to reflect on the team's performance, identify areas for improvement, and define actionable steps to enhance effectiveness and productivity in future sprints. Agile methodologies promote adaptive planning, evolutionary development, and continuous improvement, enabling teams to respond quickly to changing

requirements and deliver high-quality software that meets customer needs effectively. By embracing agile principles and practices, organizations can foster innovation, increase productivity, and achieve greater success in today's dynamic and competitive business environment.

Ideas for Study Material/Resources:
Books: "Agile Estimating and Planning" by Mike Cohn, "Scrum: The Art of Doing Twice the Work in Half the Time" by Jeff Sutherland, "Kanban: Successful Evolutionary Change for Your Technology Business" by David J. Anderson.
Online Courses: Platforms like Udemy, Coursera, and Scrum.org offer courses on agile methodologies, Scrum, Kanban, and agile project management.
Articles and Blogs: Agile blogs, project management websites, and agile communities often feature articles, case studies, and best practices for implementing agile methodologies.

Ideas for Activity:
Conduct agile workshops or simulations where participants experience agile practices, such as sprint planning, daily stand-ups, sprint reviews, and retrospectives, in a simulated project environment.
Organize agile project simulations or role-playing exercises where participants work together in cross-functional teams to plan, execute, and deliver projects using agile principles and practices.

Some Training Ideas for Facilitation:
Start by introducing participants to the principles and values of agile methodologies, such as the Agile Manifesto and the 12 Agile Principles.
Teach participants about popular agile frameworks and practices, such as Scrum, Kanban, Lean, and XP, and how they can be applied to different project scenarios.
Provide guidance on agile roles and responsibilities, agile ceremonies (e.g., sprint planning, daily stand-ups), agile artifacts (e.g., product backlog, sprint backlog), and agile metrics to measure project progress and success.

Did You Know?
Agile methodologies originated from software development practices but have since been adopted in various industries, including marketing, HR, finance, and healthcare, to improve project delivery and adaptability.

Ideas for Presentation:
Create a PowerPoint presentation or e-book summarizing key agile methodologies, principles, and practices. Include agile frameworks, ceremonies, and case studies to help learners understand and apply agile concepts effectively.

Training Video Guide:
Develop video tutorials or agile training videos explaining agile methodologies, practices, and techniques. Provide real-world examples, agile team interactions, and project simulations to help learners visualize and internalize agile concepts and practices.

Skill 52: Scrum Framework

Importance:
The Scrum framework is crucial for enabling teams to collaborate effectively, deliver value iteratively, and respond to changing requirements in complex projects. It promotes transparency, inspection, and adaptation, fostering a culture of continuous improvement and innovation.

Concept:
Scrum is an agile framework for managing and delivering complex projects, primarily in software development but applicable to various industries. It consists of roles (e.g., Product Owner, Scrum Master, Development Team), events (e.g., Sprint Planning, Daily Stand-up, Sprint Review), and artifacts (e.g., Product Backlog, Sprint Backlog, Increment) to facilitate iterative development and customer feedback.

Takeaway: Guide for Students and Professionals
By mastering the Scrum framework, individuals can lead or participate in Scrum teams to deliver high-quality products incrementally, improve team collaboration, and respond quickly to changing market needs. Scrum skills are essential for project managers, Scrum Masters, product owners, and development team members.
The Scrum framework is a widely used agile methodology for managing and developing complex products. It emphasizes collaboration, transparency, and adaptability, enabling teams to deliver value iteratively and incrementally. Here are the key components and concepts of the Scrum framework:

1. Roles :
 - Scrum Master : The Scrum Master is responsible for facilitating the Scrum process, removing impediments, and coaching the team to improve its effectiveness. They serve as servant-leaders, ensuring that the team adheres to Scrum principles and practices.
 - Product Owner : The Product Owner represents the stakeholders and is responsible for maximizing the value of the product. They define the product vision, prioritize the product backlog, and make decisions on what features to develop.
 - Development Team : The Development Team is a cross-functional group of professionals responsible for delivering potentially shippable increments of the product at the end of each sprint. They self-organize to accomplish the sprint goals and are accountable for the quality of the deliverables.

2. Artifacts :
 - Product Backlog : The Product Backlog is a prioritized list of all desired features, enhancements, and fixes for the product. It is maintained by the Product Owner and serves as the single source of requirements for the development team.
 - Sprint Backlog : The Sprint Backlog is a subset of the Product Backlog items selected for implementation in the current sprint. It contains the tasks necessary to achieve the sprint goal and is owned by the Development Team.

- Increment : The Increment is the sum of all the product backlog items completed during a sprint, including all features, enhancements, and fixes. It must be in a potentially releasable state and meet the Definition of Done.

3. Events :
   - Sprint Planning : Sprint Planning is a time-boxed meeting held at the beginning of each sprint to define the sprint goal and select the product backlog items to work on. The Development Team collaborates to create a sprint backlog and estimate effort.
   - Daily Scrum : The Daily Scrum is a short, daily meeting where the Development Team synchronizes their activities, discusses progress, and identifies any impediments. It is time-boxed to 15 minutes and is facilitated by the Scrum Master.
   - Sprint Review : Sprint Review is held at the end of each sprint to demonstrate the completed work to stakeholders and gather feedback. The Product Owner reviews the increment and discusses what was done and what remains to be done.
   - Sprint Retrospective : Sprint Retrospective is held at the end of each sprint to reflect on the team's performance, identify areas for improvement, and define actionable steps to enhance effectiveness in future sprints.

The Scrum framework promotes iterative development, continuous improvement, and collaboration among team members, enabling organizations to respond quickly to changing requirements and deliver high-quality products that meet customer needs effectively.

Ideas for Study Material/Resources:
Books: "Scrum: The Art of Doing Twice the Work in Half the Time" by Jeff Sutherland, "The Scrum Guide" by Ken Schwaber and Jeff Sutherland, "Scrum Mastery: From Good to Great Servant Leadership" by Geoff Watts.
Online Courses: Platforms like Scrum.org, Udemy, and Coursera offer courses on Scrum fundamentals, Scrum Master certification, and agile project management.
Articles and Blogs: Scrum Alliance, Scrum.org, and agile blogs often feature articles, case studies, and best practices for implementing Scrum in organizations.

Ideas for Activity:
Conduct Scrum workshops or training sessions where participants learn about Scrum roles, events, and artifacts through interactive exercises, simulations, and case studies.
Organize Scrum team simulations or role-playing exercises where participants take on different Scrum roles and practice Scrum ceremonies, such as sprint planning, daily stand-ups, and sprint reviews.

Some Training Ideas for Facilitation:
Start by introducing participants to the Scrum framework, its values (commitment, courage, focus, openness, respect), and its pillars (transparency, inspection, adaptation).
Teach participants about Scrum roles (Product Owner, Scrum Master, Development Team), events (Sprint, Sprint Planning, Daily Stand-up, Sprint Review, Sprint Retrospective), and artifacts (Product Backlog, Sprint Backlog, Increment).

Provide guidance on Scrum implementation, including establishing a product vision, creating and refining product backlogs, conducting sprint planning, managing sprint backlogs, and facilitating sprint reviews and retrospectives.

Did You Know?
The term "Scrum" originated from rugby, where it refers to a method of restarting play after an infringement, symbolizing the iterative and collaborative nature of the Scrum framework.

Ideas for Presentation:
Create a PowerPoint presentation or e-book summarizing key Scrum concepts, roles, events, and artifacts. Include visual diagrams, Scrum ceremonies, and tips for implementing Scrum effectively in organizations.

Training Video Guide:
Develop video tutorials or Scrum training videos explaining Scrum principles, roles, events, and artifacts. Provide real-world examples, Scrum team interactions, and case studies to help learners understand and apply Scrum practices in their projects.

Skill 53: Learning to Learn

Importance:
Learning to learn, also known as metacognition, is essential for acquiring new knowledge, skills, and competencies effectively. It involves understanding one's learning process, identifying learning strategies that work best, and adapting learning approaches to different subjects and contexts.

Concept:
Learning to learn encompasses the ability to set learning goals, manage time effectively, seek out relevant resources, engage in active learning strategies (such as summarizing, questioning, and self-testing), monitor one's learning progress, and reflect on learning outcomes.

Takeaway: Guide for Students and Professionals
By mastering learning-to-learn skills, individuals can become more efficient and effective learners, acquiring new knowledge and skills more quickly and retaining them for the long term. Learning-to-learn skills are essential for students, professionals, and lifelong learners seeking continuous personal and professional development.
Learning to learn, also known as metacognition, is the ability to understand and control one's own learning process. It involves developing strategies, techniques, and attitudes that enhance learning effectiveness and efficiency. Here are some key components and concepts of learning to learn:

1. Self-Awareness : Self-awareness is the foundation of learning to learn. It involves understanding one's own learning preferences, strengths, weaknesses, and areas for

improvement. By reflecting on past experiences and learning styles, individuals can identify what works best for them and adjust their approach accordingly.

2. Goal Setting : Setting clear and achievable learning goals provides direction and motivation for the learning process. By defining specific, measurable, attainable, relevant, and time-bound (SMART) goals, individuals can focus their efforts and track their progress effectively.

3. Active Learning Strategies : Active learning involves engaging with the material actively rather than passively receiving information. Techniques such as summarizing, questioning, self-testing, and teaching others can enhance understanding, retention, and application of knowledge.

4. Metacognitive Strategies : Metacognitive strategies involve monitoring and regulating one's own learning process. This includes techniques such as planning, monitoring progress, evaluating outcomes, and adjusting strategies based on feedback and results.

5. Learning Styles : Understanding different learning styles (e.g., visual, auditory, kinesthetic) can help individuals tailor their learning approach to their preferences and strengths. By incorporating activities and materials that align with their preferred learning style, individuals can optimize their learning experience.

6. Time Management : Effective time management is essential for learning to learn. It involves prioritizing tasks, allocating time for learning activities, minimizing distractions, and maintaining a balance between learning and other responsibilities.

7. Resource Management : Identifying and accessing relevant learning resources, such as books, articles, videos, courses, and online platforms, is crucial for effective learning. By leveraging a variety of resources, individuals can gain diverse perspectives and deepen their understanding of the subject matter.

8. Critical Thinking : Developing critical thinking skills enables individuals to evaluate information critically, analyze evidence, identify assumptions, and make informed decisions. By questioning, reasoning, and problem-solving, learners can enhance their ability to think critically and apply knowledge effectively.

9. Resilience and Perseverance : Learning to learn requires resilience and perseverance in the face of challenges and setbacks. Developing a growth mindset, embracing failures as opportunities for learning, and persisting in the face of difficulties are essential for continuous improvement and success.

10. Reflection and Feedback : Reflecting on learning experiences and seeking feedback from peers, mentors, or instructors can provide valuable insights and opportunities for growth. By identifying strengths, weaknesses, and areas for improvement, individuals can refine their learning strategies and enhance their overall learning effectiveness.

Learning to learn is a lifelong process that empowers individuals to become self-directed, adaptable, and lifelong learners. By cultivating metacognitive awareness, setting goals, using active learning strategies, managing time and resources effectively, and fostering critical thinking and resilience, individuals can maximize their learning potential and achieve their educational and professional goals.

Ideas for Study Material/Resources:
Books: "Make It Stick: The Science of Successful Learning" by Peter C. Brown, Henry L. Roediger III, and Mark A. McDaniel, "A Mind for Numbers: How to Excel at Math and Science (Even If You Flunked Algebra)" by Barbara Oakley, "The Art of Learning: An Inner Journey to Optimal Performance" by Josh Waitzkin.
Online Courses: Platforms like Coursera, edX, and Khan Academy offer courses on learning-to-learn skills, study strategies, and cognitive psychology.
Articles and Blogs: Educational psychology journals, learning blogs, and academic websites often feature articles and research studies on effective learning strategies and study techniques.

Ideas for Activity:
Conduct learning-to-learn workshops or seminars where participants explore different learning strategies, such as spaced repetition, retrieval practice, and elaborative interrogation, and apply them to their own learning goals.
Organize peer-learning groups or study circles where participants collaborate to share learning resources, discuss study techniques, and provide feedback on each other's learning approaches.

Some Training Ideas for Facilitation:
Start by introducing participants to the concept of learning to learn and its importance in academic and professional contexts.
Teach participants about effective learning strategies and study techniques, such as active recall, interleaved practice, and distributed practice, supported by research in cognitive psychology.
Provide guidance on setting SMART learning goals, managing time effectively, creating study schedules, and using learning resources efficiently to optimize the learning process.

Did You Know?
Metacognitive strategies, such as self-questioning and self-monitoring, can significantly enhance learning outcomes by helping learners regulate their cognitive processes and adapt their learning strategies to different tasks and challenges.

Ideas for Presentation:
Create a PowerPoint presentation or e-book summarizing key learning-to-learn concepts, strategies, and techniques. Include visual aids, mnemonic devices, and real-life examples to help learners understand and apply effective learning strategies.

Training Video Guide:
Develop video tutorials or learning-to-learn videos demonstrating different learning strategies, study techniques, and metacognitive skills. Provide practical tips, case

studies, and examples of successful learning experiences to inspire and motivate learners to improve their learning skills.

Skill 54: Risk Management

Importance:
Risk management is crucial for identifying, assessing, and mitigating potential risks that may impact the success of projects, initiatives, or organizations. It involves analyzing uncertainties, developing risk response strategies, and monitoring risk factors to minimize negative impacts and maximize opportunities.

Concept:
Risk management encompasses the process of identifying, analyzing, prioritizing, and responding to risks proactively. It involves risk identification techniques (such as brainstorming and SWOT analysis), risk assessment methodologies (such as qualitative and quantitative analysis), and risk mitigation strategies (such as risk avoidance, risk transfer, risk reduction, and risk acceptance).

Takeaway: Guide for Students and Professionals
By mastering risk management skills, individuals can anticipate potential threats and opportunities, develop contingency plans, and make informed decisions to protect assets, achieve objectives, and enhance organizational resilience. Risk management skills are essential for project managers, business leaders, and risk professionals across industries.

Risk management is the process of identifying, assessing, and mitigating risks to minimize potential negative impacts and maximize opportunities for success. It involves analyzing potential threats and uncertainties, evaluating their likelihood and impact, and implementing strategies to manage or mitigate them effectively. Here are key components and concepts of risk management:

1.   Risk Identification : Risk identification involves identifying potential threats or opportunities that could affect the achievement of objectives. This includes internal and external factors such as market volatility, regulatory changes, technology failures, natural disasters, and human error.

2. Risk Assessment : Risk assessment evaluates the likelihood and impact of identified risks to determine their significance and prioritize them for further analysis. This may involve qualitative assessments (e.g., risk matrices, risk registers) or quantitative assessments (e.g., Monte Carlo simulations, probabilistic models) to quantify risks more precisely.

3.   Risk Analysis : Risk analysis examines the characteristics and potential consequences of identified risks to develop a deeper understanding of their nature and implications. This may involve analyzing the root causes of risks, their interdependencies, and the potential cascading effects on projects, processes, or organizations.

4. Risk Evaluation : Risk evaluation compares the assessed risks against predefined risk criteria (e.g., risk appetite, risk tolerance) to determine their acceptability and inform decision-making. Risks may be categorized as acceptable, tolerable, unacceptable, or requiring further treatment based on their likelihood and impact.

5. Risk Treatment : Risk treatment involves developing and implementing strategies to address identified risks effectively. This may include risk mitigation (reducing the likelihood or impact of risks), risk avoidance (eliminating the risk altogether), risk transfer (shifting the risk to another party through insurance or contracts), or risk acceptance (acknowledging and managing the risk without further action).

6. Risk Monitoring : Risk monitoring involves tracking and reviewing the effectiveness of risk management activities over time. It includes regular monitoring of risk indicators, triggers, and thresholds to detect changes in risk levels, emerging risks, or deviations from planned risk responses.

7. Contingency Planning : Contingency planning involves developing alternative courses of action to address unforeseen events or changes in circumstances that could impact the achievement of objectives. This may include establishing contingency reserves, fallback plans, or crisis management protocols to respond effectively to unexpected risks or disruptions.

8. Risk Communication : Risk communication involves sharing information about risks, their potential impacts, and risk management strategies with stakeholders to facilitate informed decision-making and promote transparency. Effective communication ensures that stakeholders are aware of risks and engaged in risk management efforts.

9. Risk Culture : Risk culture refers to the attitudes, values, and behaviors within an organization regarding risk awareness, accountability, and responsiveness. A strong risk culture fosters proactive risk management practices, encourages open communication, and empowers individuals to identify and address risks effectively.

10. Continuous Improvement : Continuous improvement involves evaluating and refining risk management processes and practices based on lessons learned, feedback, and performance metrics. It promotes a culture of learning, adaptation, and resilience, enabling organizations to enhance their risk management capabilities over time.

By implementing robust risk management processes and practices, organizations can identify and address potential threats, capitalize on opportunities, and achieve their objectives with greater confidence and resilience. Effective risk management enables organizations to navigate uncertainty, make informed decisions, and sustain long-term success in a dynamic and evolving business environment.

Ideas for Study Material/Resources:
Books: "The Essentials of Risk Management" by Michel Crouhy, Dan Galai, and Robert Mark, "Risk Management: Concepts and Guidance" by Carl L. Pritchard, "The Black Swan: The Impact of the Highly Improbable" by Nassim Nicholas Taleb.

Online Courses: Platforms like Udemy, Coursera, and Project Management Institute (PMI) offer courses on risk management fundamentals, project risk analysis, and risk assessment techniques.

Articles and Blogs: Risk management journals, project management websites, and risk analysis blogs often feature articles, case studies, and best practices for managing risks effectively.

Ideas for Activity:
Conduct risk management workshops or tabletop exercises where participants identify, assess, and prioritize risks for hypothetical projects or scenarios, and develop risk response plans collaboratively.

Organize risk assessment sessions or risk analysis simulations where participants analyze real-world risk scenarios, such as market risks, operational risks, or cybersecurity risks, and propose risk mitigation strategies.

Some Training Ideas for Facilitation:
Start by introducing participants to the concepts and principles of risk management, including risk identification, risk analysis, risk evaluation, and risk treatment.

Teach participants about risk management frameworks, such as ISO 31000, COSO ERM, and PMI's Project Risk Management framework, and how they can be applied to different industries and projects.

Provide guidance on conducting risk assessments, performing risk analysis techniques (such as probability and impact assessment, Monte Carlo simulation), developing risk registers, and implementing risk response plans.

Did You Know?
Risk management is not only about mitigating negative risks (threats) but also about maximizing positive risks (opportunities) to achieve strategic objectives and gain competitive advantages.

Ideas for Presentation:
Create a PowerPoint presentation or e-book summarizing key risk management concepts, methodologies, and best practices. Include risk management frameworks, risk assessment tools, and case studies to help learners understand and apply risk management principles effectively.

Training Video Guide:
Develop video tutorials or risk management videos explaining risk management processes, techniques, and case studies. Provide practical examples, risk analysis demonstrations, and tips for effective risk management in various organizational contexts.

Skill 55: Supply Chain Management

Importance:
Supply chain management (SCM) is crucial for optimizing the flow of goods and services from raw material suppliers to end customers efficiently. It involves planning,

sourcing, producing, and delivering products or services while minimizing costs, maximizing value, and meeting customer demand.

Concept:
Supply chain management encompasses the coordination and integration of key business processes across the supply chain, including procurement, logistics, production, inventory management, and distribution. It aims to streamline operations, reduce lead times, manage risks, and enhance overall supply chain performance.

Takeaway: Guide for Students and Professionals
By mastering supply chain management skills, individuals can optimize supply chain operations, reduce costs, improve customer satisfaction, and gain a competitive advantage in the marketplace. Supply chain management skills are essential for supply chain managers, logistics professionals, procurement specialists, and operations managers.
Supply chain management (SCM) is the strategic coordination of activities involved in the sourcing, production, transportation, and distribution of goods and services from suppliers to customers. It encompasses the planning, execution, and optimization of all processes involved in delivering products or services to end-users while maximizing efficiency and minimizing costs. Here are key components and concepts of supply chain management:

1.   Supply Chain Planning : Supply chain planning involves forecasting demand, developing production schedules, and determining inventory levels to meet customer demand efficiently. It includes strategic planning, demand planning, production planning, and inventory planning to optimize resource allocation and minimize supply chain disruptions.

2. Supplier Relationship Management (SRM) : SRM focuses on managing relationships with suppliers to ensure a reliable and cost-effective supply of materials and components. It includes supplier selection, contract negotiation, performance evaluation, and collaboration to improve quality, delivery, and cost efficiency.

3. Inventory Management : Inventory management involves controlling the flow of materials and goods throughout the supply chain to balance supply and demand effectively. It includes inventory optimization, safety stock management, and inventory tracking to minimize stockouts, reduce carrying costs, and improve customer service levels.

4.   Logistics and Transportation : Logistics and transportation encompass the movement of goods from suppliers to manufacturers, warehouses, distribution centers, and ultimately to customers. It involves selecting transportation modes, routing shipments, optimizing freight costs, and managing transportation networks to ensure timely delivery and reduce transportation expenses.

5. Warehousing and Distribution : Warehousing and distribution involve the storage, handling, and distribution of goods within the supply chain network. It includes warehouse design, layout optimization, order picking, packing, and shipping to

streamline operations, minimize inventory holding costs, and improve order fulfillment efficiency.

6. Demand Management : Demand management focuses on understanding and influencing customer demand to optimize inventory levels and production capacity. It includes demand forecasting, demand shaping, and demand sensing to anticipate market trends, adjust production plans, and align supply with demand more effectively.

7. Supplier Collaboration and Integration : Supplier collaboration and integration involve sharing information, coordinating activities, and aligning processes with key suppliers to enhance visibility, agility, and responsiveness across the supply chain. It includes implementing collaborative planning, forecasting, and replenishment (CPFR) initiatives, as well as integrating systems and processes for seamless communication and coordination.

8. Risk Management : Risk management in supply chain management involves identifying, assessing, and mitigating risks that could disrupt operations or impact supply chain performance. It includes analyzing potential risks such as supply chain disruptions, geopolitical issues, natural disasters, and market fluctuations, as well as implementing strategies to manage and mitigate these risks effectively.

9. Sustainability and Corporate Social Responsibility (CSR) : Sustainability and CSR initiatives in supply chain management focus on promoting ethical, environmentally responsible, and socially sustainable practices throughout the supply chain. It includes sourcing materials ethically, reducing carbon emissions, minimizing waste, and ensuring fair labor practices to create value for all stakeholders and contribute to a more sustainable future.

10. Supply Chain Analytics and Technology : Supply chain analytics and technology involve leveraging data, analytics, and digital technologies to optimize supply chain performance, enhance decision-making, and drive continuous improvement. It includes using advanced analytics, artificial intelligence (AI), blockchain, Internet of Things (IoT), and supply chain management software to increase visibility, agility, and efficiency throughout the supply chain.

By effectively managing these key components and concepts of supply chain management, organizations can optimize their supply chain performance, reduce costs, improve customer satisfaction, and gain a competitive advantage in today's global marketplace. Supply chain management plays a critical role in enabling organizations to adapt to changing market conditions, mitigate risks, and achieve sustainable growth and success over the long term.

Ideas for Study Material/Resources:
Books: "Introduction to Materials Management" by J.R. Tony Arnold, Stephen N. Chapman, and Lloyd M. Clive, "Supply Chain Management: Strategy, Planning, and Operation" by Sunil Chopra and Peter Meindl, "The New Science of Retailing: How

Analytics Are Transforming the Supply Chain and Improving Performance" by Marshall Fisher and Ananth Raman.
Online Courses: Platforms like Coursera, edX, and MIT OpenCourseWare offer courses on supply chain management fundamentals, logistics and transportation, inventory management, and supply chain analytics.
Articles and Blogs: Supply chain management journals, logistics magazines, and industry-specific websites often feature articles, case studies, and best practices for optimizing supply chain operations.

Ideas for Activity:
Conduct supply chain management simulations or case studies where participants analyze real-world supply chain scenarios, identify bottlenecks, and develop strategies to improve supply chain performance.
Organize supply chain optimization workshops or Kaizen events where participants collaborate to streamline supply chain processes, reduce waste, and implement continuous improvement initiatives.

Some Training Ideas for Facilitation:
Start by introducing participants to the key components of the supply chain, including suppliers, manufacturers, distributors, retailers, and customers, and the flow of materials, information, and finances.
Teach participants about supply chain management strategies, such as lean manufacturing, just-in-time (JIT) inventory, vendor-managed inventory (VMI), and agile supply chain, and how they can be applied to different industries and contexts.
Provide guidance on supply chain planning, demand forecasting, inventory optimization, warehouse management, transportation logistics, and supply chain risk management.

Did You Know?
Supply chain disruptions, such as natural disasters, geopolitical conflicts, or global pandemics, can have significant impacts on supply chain performance, highlighting the importance of supply chain resilience and risk mitigation strategies.

Ideas for Presentation:
Create a PowerPoint presentation or e-book summarizing key supply chain management concepts, strategies, and best practices. Include supply chain diagrams, process maps, and case studies to help learners visualize and understand supply chain principles effectively.

Training Video Guide:
Develop video tutorials or supply chain management videos explaining supply chain processes, techniques, and case studies. Provide real-world examples, supply chain simulations, and interviews with industry experts to illustrate supply chain management principles in action.

Skill 56: Logistics and Inventory Management

Importance:
Logistics and inventory management are essential components of supply chain management, focusing on the efficient flow and storage of goods from suppliers to customers. Effective logistics and inventory management ensure timely delivery, optimal inventory levels, and cost-efficient operations.

Concept:
Logistics involves the planning, implementation, and control of the movement and storage of goods, services, and information within the supply chain. Inventory management focuses on overseeing the ordering, storage, and tracking of inventory to meet customer demand while minimizing carrying costs and stockouts.

Takeaway: Guide for Students and Professionals
By mastering logistics and inventory management skills, individuals can optimize transportation, warehousing, and inventory processes, reduce lead times, minimize inventory carrying costs, and improve customer service levels. These skills are essential for logistics managers, warehouse supervisors, inventory planners, and supply chain professionals.

Logistics and inventory management are integral components of supply chain management, focusing on the efficient movement, storage, and control of goods throughout the supply chain. Here are key components and concepts of logistics and inventory management:

1. Transportation Management : Transportation management involves planning, coordinating, and optimizing the movement of goods from suppliers to customers. It includes selecting transportation modes (e.g., trucking, rail, air, sea), routing shipments, scheduling deliveries, and managing transportation networks to ensure timely and cost-effective delivery.

2. Warehousing and Storage : Warehousing and storage encompass the physical handling, storage, and management of inventory within distribution centers or warehouses. It includes warehouse design, layout optimization, inventory storage methods (e.g., shelving, pallets, racks), and material handling equipment (e.g., forklifts, conveyors) to maximize space utilization and streamline operations.

3. Inventory Control and Optimization : Inventory control and optimization involve managing inventory levels to balance supply and demand effectively while minimizing holding costs and stockouts. It includes inventory forecasting, demand planning, safety stock management, and inventory replenishment strategies (e.g., Just-in-Time, Economic Order Quantity) to ensure adequate stock availability and reduce excess inventory.

4. Order Fulfillment and Processing : Order fulfillment and processing encompass the activities involved in receiving, processing, picking, packing, and shipping customer orders. It includes order management systems, picking technologies (e.g., batch

picking, zone picking), packing materials, and shipping carriers to fulfill orders accurately and efficiently while meeting customer service level agreements.

5. Cross-Docking and Transshipment : Cross-docking and transshipment strategies involve transferring goods directly from inbound to outbound transportation vehicles without intermediate storage. It helps reduce inventory holding costs, minimize handling, and improve order cycle times by streamlining the flow of goods through distribution centers.

6. Reverse Logistics : Reverse logistics deals with the management of returned or defective products, including product recalls, repairs, recycling, or disposal. It involves reverse supply chain processes, such as returns management, refurbishment, recycling, and disposition, to recover value from returned goods and minimize environmental impact.

7. Inventory Visibility and Tracking : Inventory visibility and tracking enable real-time monitoring and tracking of inventory throughout the supply chain. It includes inventory management systems, barcode scanning, RFID (Radio Frequency Identification) technology, and IoT (Internet of Things) sensors to provide visibility into inventory levels, location, and movement across multiple locations and distribution channels.

8. Inventory Accuracy and Cycle Counting : Inventory accuracy is crucial for effective inventory management, ensuring that physical inventory matches recorded inventory levels. Cycle counting involves regularly counting a portion of inventory items to verify accuracy, identify discrepancies, and maintain inventory integrity without disrupting operations.

9. Vendor Managed Inventory (VMI) : Vendor Managed Inventory (VMI) is a collaborative inventory management approach where suppliers monitor and replenish inventory levels at customer locations based on predefined agreements. It helps optimize inventory levels, reduce stockouts, and improve supply chain efficiency by shifting inventory management responsibilities to suppliers.

10. Inventory Optimization Software : Inventory optimization software utilizes advanced algorithms and analytics to optimize inventory levels, reduce costs, and improve service levels. It includes inventory management systems, demand forecasting tools, and supply chain planning software to analyze demand patterns, forecast future demand, and optimize inventory replenishment decisions.

By effectively managing logistics and inventory, organizations can improve supply chain efficiency, reduce costs, enhance customer satisfaction, and gain a competitive advantage in today's dynamic and demanding marketplace. Logistics and inventory management play a critical role in optimizing supply chain performance, ensuring the smooth flow of goods, and meeting customer expectations effectively.

Ideas for Study Material/Resources:
Books: "Logistics and Supply Chain Management" by Martin Christopher, "Inventory Management Explained: A Focus on Forecasting, Lot Sizing, Safety Stock, and Ordering Systems" by David J. Piasecki, "The Handbook of Logistics and Distribution Management" by Alan Rushton, Phil Croucher, and Peter Baker.
Online Courses: Platforms like Coursera, LinkedIn Learning, and MIT OpenCourseWare offer courses on logistics management, inventory control, warehouse operations, and transportation logistics.
Articles and Blogs: Logistics and supply chain management journals, industry magazines, and logistics websites often feature articles, case studies, and best practices for improving logistics and inventory management.

Ideas for Activity:
Conduct logistics and inventory management simulations or case studies where participants analyze real-world logistics scenarios, optimize transportation routes, and develop inventory replenishment strategies.
Organize warehouse layout optimization workshops or gemba walks where participants identify inefficiencies in warehouse operations, such as stockouts, overstocking, and inefficient layout, and propose improvements.

Some Training Ideas for Facilitation:
Start by introducing participants to the concepts and principles of logistics and inventory management, including transportation modes, warehouse operations, inventory control techniques, and order fulfillment processes.
Teach participants about logistics planning, route optimization, inventory forecasting, demand planning, safety stock management, ABC analysis, and inventory optimization models.
Provide guidance on warehouse management systems (WMS), inventory management software, barcode technology, RFID systems, and other tools used in logistics and inventory management.

Did You Know?
Effective inventory management involves balancing conflicting objectives, such as minimizing holding costs (carrying costs) while ensuring sufficient inventory levels to meet customer demand and avoid stockouts.

Ideas for Presentation:
Create a PowerPoint presentation or e-book summarizing key logistics and inventory management concepts, techniques, and best practices. Include flowcharts, process diagrams, and case studies to help learners understand and apply logistics and inventory management principles effectively.

Training Video Guide:
Develop video tutorials or logistics and inventory management videos explaining logistics processes, inventory control techniques, and warehouse management practices. Provide visual demonstrations, real-world examples, and interviews with industry experts to illustrate key concepts and strategies.

Skill 57: Health and Safety Regulations

Importance:
Health and safety regulations are essential for ensuring the well-being and protection of employees, customers, and the public in various workplaces and environments. Compliance with health and safety regulations helps prevent accidents, injuries, and illnesses, promoting a safe and healthy work environment.

Concept:
Health and safety regulations encompass legal requirements, standards, and guidelines established by government agencies and regulatory bodies to protect individuals from hazards and risks in the workplace. They cover areas such as workplace safety, occupational health, emergency preparedness, and environmental protection.

Takeaway: Guide for Students and Professionals
By mastering health and safety regulations, individuals can create and maintain safe working environments, prevent workplace accidents and injuries, and comply with legal requirements and industry standards. Health and safety skills are essential for employers, managers, supervisors, and employees across industries.
Health and safety regulations are laws and standards designed to protect the well-being of workers and the public by ensuring safe working conditions and minimizing the risk of accidents, injuries, and occupational illnesses. These regulations are enforced by government agencies and regulatory bodies to establish minimum requirements for workplace safety and health. Here are key components and concepts of health and safety regulations:

1. Occupational Health and Safety Act (OSHA) : The Occupational Safety and Health Act (OSHA) is a federal law in the United States that sets forth standards for workplace safety and health. It requires employers to provide a safe and healthful work environment for employees by identifying and mitigating hazards, providing training, and complying with OSHA standards.

2. Regulatory Agencies : Regulatory agencies, such as the Occupational Safety and Health Administration (OSHA) in the United States, are responsible for enforcing health and safety regulations and conducting inspections to ensure compliance with safety standards. These agencies may also provide guidance, training, and assistance to employers and employees to promote workplace safety.

3. Safety Standards and Regulations : Safety standards and regulations establish specific requirements for workplace safety, including hazard communication, personal protective equipment (PPE), electrical safety, machine guarding, fall protection, and hazardous materials handling. These standards are based on industry best practices, scientific research, and consensus standards developed by organizations such as the American National Standards Institute (ANSI) and the National Fire Protection Association (NFPA).

4. Risk Assessment and Hazard Identification : Employers are required to assess workplace hazards, identify potential risks, and implement controls to mitigate or eliminate hazards that could cause harm to employees. This includes conducting risk assessments, safety inspections, and job hazard analyses to identify hazards and develop appropriate control measures.

5. Safety Training and Education : Employers are responsible for providing safety training and education to employees to ensure they are aware of workplace hazards, know how to safely perform their job duties, and understand emergency procedures. Training topics may include hazard recognition, PPE use, emergency response, and safety procedures specific to the workplace.

6. Recordkeeping and Reporting : Employers are required to maintain records of workplace injuries, illnesses, and incidents, as well as safety training documentation, safety inspections, and hazard assessments. They must also report certain workplace injuries, illnesses, and fatalities to regulatory agencies as required by law.

7. Emergency Preparedness and Response : Employers must develop and implement emergency preparedness and response plans to address potential emergencies, such as fires, chemical spills, natural disasters, and medical emergencies. These plans should include procedures for evacuation, first aid, communication, and coordination with emergency responders.

8. Worker Rights and Responsibilities : Workers have the right to a safe and healthful work environment and the responsibility to follow safety rules and procedures established by their employer. They also have the right to report unsafe conditions or concerns to their employer or regulatory agencies without fear of retaliation.

9. Enforcement and Penalties : Regulatory agencies have the authority to enforce health and safety regulations through inspections, citations, fines, and penalties for non-compliance. Employers found to be in violation of safety standards may face monetary penalties, citations, and enforcement actions to ensure corrective actions are taken to address hazards and improve workplace safety.

10. Continuous Improvement : Health and safety regulations promote a culture of continuous improvement by requiring employers to regularly evaluate and improve their safety programs, hazard controls, and safety management systems. Employers are encouraged to involve employees in safety committees, safety inspections, and safety improvement initiatives to identify opportunities for enhancing workplace safety and health.

By complying with health and safety regulations, employers can protect the well-being of their employees, reduce the risk of workplace injuries and illnesses, and create a safer and healthier work environment for all stakeholders. Health and safety regulations play a vital role in promoting workplace safety, preventing accidents, and safeguarding the health and well-being of workers and the public.

Ideas for Study Material/Resources:
Books: "Occupational Health and Safety Management: A Practical Approach" by Charles D. Reese, "Introduction to Health and Safety in Construction" by Phil Hughes and Ed Ferrett, "The Complete Guide to OSHA Compliance" by Joel M. Cohen.
Online Courses: Platforms like Coursera, Udemy, and Occupational Safety and Health Administration (OSHA) offer courses on occupational health and safety, workplace safety regulations, and safety management systems.
Articles and Blogs: Occupational health and safety journals, safety blogs, and government websites provide articles, guides, and resources on health and safety regulations and best practices.

Ideas for Activity:
Conduct workplace safety audits or inspections where participants assess workplace hazards, identify non-compliance issues, and develop corrective action plans to address safety deficiencies.
Organize safety training sessions or toolbox talks where participants learn about specific health and safety regulations, emergency procedures, personal protective equipment (PPE) usage, and hazard communication.

Some Training Ideas for Facilitation:
Start by introducing participants to the importance of health and safety regulations and their legal obligations to maintain a safe work environment.
Teach participants about relevant health and safety laws, regulations, and standards applicable to their industry or workplace, such as Occupational Safety and Health Act (OSHA) regulations, Environmental Protection Agency (EPA) regulations, and National Fire Protection Association (NFPA) codes.
Provide guidance on conducting risk assessments, developing safety management systems, implementing safety policies and procedures, and training employees on health and safety practices.

Did You Know?
Effective health and safety management involves a proactive approach, including hazard identification, risk assessment, hazard control, employee training, and continuous improvement.

Ideas for Presentation:
Create a PowerPoint presentation or e-book summarizing key health and safety regulations, standards, and best practices. Include visuals, infographics, and case studies to illustrate compliance requirements and safety management principles effectively.

Training Video Guide:
Develop video tutorials or health and safety training videos explaining health and safety regulations, hazard recognition, and safety procedures. Provide real-life scenarios, workplace simulations, and demonstrations of safety practices to reinforce learning and promote compliance.

Skill 58: First Aid/CPR

Importance:
First aid and CPR (Cardiopulmonary Resuscitation) skills are crucial for providing immediate assistance to individuals experiencing medical emergencies, such as cardiac arrest, choking, or injuries. Prompt and effective first aid and CPR interventions can save lives and prevent further harm until professional medical help arrives.

Concept:
First aid involves the initial care and treatment provided to someone who is injured or suddenly ill until medical professionals arrive. CPR is a life-saving technique used to maintain blood circulation and oxygenation when a person's heart has stopped beating or when they are not breathing effectively.

Takeaway: Guide for Students and Professionals
By mastering first aid and CPR skills, individuals can respond confidently and effectively to medical emergencies, assess the situation, provide appropriate first aid interventions, and perform CPR when necessary. First aid and CPR skills are essential for individuals in both personal and professional settings.
First Aid and Cardiopulmonary Resuscitation (CPR) are critical skills that can save lives in emergency situations by providing immediate care and support to individuals who are injured or experiencing medical emergencies. Here are key components and concepts of First Aid and CPR:

1. Basic First Aid : Basic First Aid involves providing initial care and treatment to individuals who are injured or suddenly ill until professional medical help arrives. It includes assessing the scene for safety, checking the person's responsiveness, and administering appropriate first aid interventions based on the nature of the injury or illness.

2. CPR (Cardiopulmonary Resuscitation) : CPR is an emergency procedure performed to manually maintain circulation and oxygenation in individuals experiencing cardiac arrest or sudden cardiac arrest. It involves chest compressions to circulate blood and rescue breaths to provide oxygen until advanced medical help arrives.

3. Chain of Survival : The Chain of Survival is a series of actions that, when performed promptly and effectively, can improve the chances of survival for individuals experiencing cardiac arrest. It includes early recognition and activation of the emergency response system, early CPR, rapid defibrillation, and advanced medical care.

4. Recognizing Signs of Medical Emergencies : First aid and CPR training teach individuals how to recognize signs and symptoms of common medical emergencies, such as heart attack, stroke, choking, allergic reactions, and respiratory distress. Early recognition of these emergencies enables prompt intervention and improves outcomes.

5. Safety and Scene Assessment : Safety is paramount in providing first aid and CPR. Training emphasizes the importance of assessing the scene for potential hazards and ensuring personal safety before providing assistance to the injured or ill person. This includes assessing for dangers such as traffic, fire, or chemical hazards.

6. Airway Management : Maintaining an open airway is critical in CPR and first aid. Training covers techniques for opening and maintaining the airway, including head-tilt/chin-lift maneuver, jaw thrust maneuver (for suspected neck injuries), and clearing obstructions from the airway to ensure adequate breathing.

7. Bleeding Control and Wound Care : First aid training includes techniques for controlling bleeding and providing basic wound care. This may involve applying direct pressure to wounds, elevating injured limbs, and using dressings or bandages to cover and protect wounds from contamination.

8. Shock Management : Shock is a life-threatening condition that can occur as a result of severe injury or illness. First aid training teaches individuals how to recognize signs of shock (e.g., pale, clammy skin, rapid heartbeat) and how to manage shock by maintaining body warmth, elevating the legs, and seeking medical help promptly.

9. AED (Automated External Defibrillator) Use : AEDs are portable devices that deliver an electric shock to restore normal heart rhythm in individuals experiencing sudden cardiac arrest. CPR training often includes instruction on how to use an AED safely and effectively, including how to attach electrode pads and deliver shocks.

10. Certification and Recertification : Training in first aid and CPR typically leads to certification, which demonstrates competency in providing emergency care. Certification may require periodic recertification to ensure that individuals maintain their skills and knowledge up to date.

By learning and practicing first aid and CPR skills, individuals can become empowered to respond effectively to emergencies, provide immediate assistance to those in need, and potentially save lives. First aid and CPR training play a crucial role in building resilient and prepared communities, where individuals are equipped to respond confidently and competently in times of crisis.

Ideas for Study Material/Resources:
Books: "First Aid Manual" by British Red Cross, "CPR and AED: A Pocket Guide" by Alton L. Thygerson and Steven M. Thygerson, "Emergency First Response Primary Care (CPR) Participant Manual" by Emergency First Response Corp.
Online Courses: Platforms like American Red Cross, American Heart Association, and St. John Ambulance offer online first aid and CPR courses with interactive modules, videos, and certification options.
Articles and Blogs: First aid and CPR blogs, health websites, and medical organizations provide articles, guides, and resources on first aid techniques, CPR protocols, and emergency response procedures.

Ideas for Activity:
Conduct first aid and CPR training sessions or workshops where participants learn and practice basic first aid techniques, such as wound care, bandaging, splinting, and CPR compressions and breaths.

Organize scenario-based simulations or role-playing exercises where participants respond to simulated medical emergencies, assess patient conditions, and apply first aid and CPR skills in real-life scenarios.

Some Training Ideas for Facilitation:
Start by introducing participants to the principles of first aid and CPR, including the ABCs of first aid (Airway, Breathing, Circulation), primary survey, secondary survey, and basic life support (BLS) protocols.

Teach participants how to recognize common medical emergencies, such as heart attacks, strokes, choking incidents, and traumatic injuries, and provide appropriate first aid interventions and CPR techniques.

Provide hands-on training and practice sessions, using manikins and simulation equipment, to reinforce first aid and CPR skills and build confidence in performing life-saving interventions.

Did You Know?
Immediate bystander intervention with CPR can double or triple a cardiac arrest victim's chance of survival until emergency medical services arrive.

Ideas for Presentation:
Create a PowerPoint presentation or e-book summarizing key first aid and CPR techniques, procedures, and guidelines. Include step-by-step instructions, illustrations, and mnemonic aids to help learners remember and apply first aid and CPR skills effectively.

Training Video Guide:
Develop video tutorials or first aid and CPR training videos demonstrating first aid techniques, CPR compressions, and rescue breaths. Provide visual demonstrations, case studies, and scenarios to illustrate proper first aid and CPR procedures and reinforce learning.

Skill 59: Foreign Language Proficiency

Importance:
Foreign language proficiency is essential in today's interconnected world, enabling individuals to communicate effectively with people from different cultures and backgrounds. Proficiency in foreign languages enhances cultural understanding, facilitates international business transactions, and opens up opportunities for personal and professional growth.

Concept:
Foreign language proficiency involves the ability to understand, speak, read, and write in languages other than one's native language. It encompasses vocabulary, grammar,

pronunciation, and cultural nuances necessary for effective communication in diverse linguistic contexts.

Takeaway: Guide for Students and Professionals
By mastering foreign language proficiency, individuals can expand their global communication skills, build cross-cultural relationships, pursue international career opportunities, and navigate multicultural environments with confidence and sensitivity.
Foreign language proficiency refers to the ability to communicate effectively in a language other than one's native language. Proficiency levels can range from basic to advanced, depending on the individual's ability to understand, speak, read, and write in the foreign language. Here are key components and concepts of foreign language proficiency:

1. Language Skills : Language proficiency encompasses four primary skills: listening, speaking, reading, and writing. Proficiency in each skill area may vary depending on the individual's exposure to and practice with the language.

2. Vocabulary and Grammar : Vocabulary refers to the words and phrases used in a language, while grammar encompasses the rules and structures governing how those words are used in sentences. Proficiency in vocabulary and grammar is essential for effective communication in a foreign language.

3. Comprehension : Comprehension is the ability to understand spoken or written language. Proficient language learners can comprehend conversations, lectures, articles, or texts in the target language, even when dealing with unfamiliar topics or vocabulary.

4. Expression : Expression involves the ability to communicate ideas, thoughts, and emotions effectively in the target language. Proficient language users can express themselves clearly and coherently through spoken or written communication.

5. Cultural Competence : Cultural competence refers to understanding and respecting the cultural norms, customs, and practices associated with the target language. Proficient language learners not only understand the language itself but also appreciate the cultural context in which it is used.

6. Language Proficiency Levels : Language proficiency levels are often categorized into standardized scales, such as the Common European Framework of Reference for Languages (CEFR) or the American Council on the Teaching of Foreign Languages (ACTFL) proficiency guidelines. These scales typically include levels such as A1 (beginner), A2 (elementary), B1 (intermediate), B2 (upper-intermediate), C1 (advanced), and C2 (proficient/native-like).

7. Language Proficiency Tests : Language proficiency tests assess individuals' language skills and determine their proficiency level in the target language. Common language proficiency tests include the Test of English as a Foreign Language (TOEFL), the

International English Language Testing System (IELTS), and the Diplôme d'études en langue française (DELF) for French proficiency.

8. Language Learning Strategies : Language learning strategies are techniques and approaches used to acquire and improve foreign language skills. Effective language learners may employ strategies such as vocabulary building, grammar practice, language immersion, language exchange, and cultural immersion to enhance their proficiency.

9. Language Immersion Programs : Language immersion programs provide opportunities for individuals to immerse themselves in the target language and culture, typically through immersive experiences such as study abroad programs, language camps, or language exchange programs. Immersion programs can accelerate language learning and enhance proficiency by providing real-world exposure to the language.

10. Lifelong Learning : Language proficiency is a lifelong journey that requires continuous practice and improvement. Proficient language users engage in lifelong learning activities such as reading, listening to podcasts, watching films, participating in conversation groups, or taking language classes to maintain and enhance their language skills over time.

By developing foreign language proficiency, individuals can broaden their horizons, enhance their career prospects, and connect with people and cultures around the world. Proficiency in a foreign language opens doors to opportunities for travel, work, study, and personal enrichment, allowing individuals to communicate effectively and engage meaningfully in a globalized world.

Ideas for Study Material/Resources:
Books: Language textbooks, grammar guides, and bilingual dictionaries tailored to specific languages, such as "Pimsleur Spanish," "Genki: An Integrated Course in Elementary Japanese," or "Assimil German."
Online Courses: Platforms like Duolingo, Rosetta Stone, and Babbel offer interactive online courses in various languages, ranging from beginner to advanced levels.
Language Learning Apps: Mobile apps like Memrise, FluentU, and HelloTalk provide language learning exercises, flashcards, and conversation practice opportunities on-the-go.
Language Exchange Communities: Websites like Tandem, iTalki, and Conversation Exchange facilitate language exchange partnerships with native speakers for practicing conversation and language skills.

Ideas for Activity:
Engage in language immersion experiences, such as language study abroad programs, cultural exchanges, or virtual language meetups, to practice speaking and listening skills in authentic contexts.
Utilize language learning apps and online platforms to participate in language challenges, quizzes, and interactive exercises to reinforce vocabulary, grammar, and pronunciation skills.

Some Training Ideas for Facilitation:
Start by setting language learning goals and selecting a target language based on personal interests, career objectives, or travel plans.
Incorporate a variety of language learning methods and resources, including textbooks, online courses, language apps, podcasts, and language exchange programs, to cater to different learning styles and preferences.
Emphasize regular practice, consistency, and immersion in the target language through listening, speaking, reading, and writing activities to improve overall language proficiency.

Did You Know?
Learning a foreign language has cognitive benefits, such as improved memory, multitasking abilities, problem-solving skills, and enhanced creativity.

Ideas for Presentation:
Create a PowerPoint presentation or e-book providing an overview of language learning strategies, resources, and tips for developing foreign language proficiency. Include cultural insights, language learning milestones, and success stories to motivate and inspire learners.

Training Video Guide:
Develop video tutorials or language learning videos demonstrating pronunciation techniques, grammar rules, and language learning strategies specific to the target language. Incorporate real-life dialogues, cultural insights, and language immersion experiences to enhance learning and engagement.

Skill 60: Spreadsheet Software (e.g., Excel)

Importance:
Proficiency in spreadsheet software, such as Microsoft Excel, is essential for data analysis, financial modeling, project management, and various administrative tasks in both personal and professional settings. Excel skills are highly valued in many industries and roles, including finance, accounting, marketing, and operations.

Concept:
Spreadsheet software allows users to organize, analyze, and visualize data in tabular formats, using features like formulas, functions, charts, and pivot tables. Proficiency in Excel involves understanding its interface, basic and advanced functions, data manipulation techniques, and formatting options.

Takeaway: Guide for Students and Professionals
By mastering spreadsheet software skills, individuals can streamline data management tasks, perform complex calculations, create informative visualizations, and make data-driven decisions with accuracy and efficiency. Excel proficiency is a valuable asset for professionals seeking to enhance their productivity and analytical capabilities.

Spreadsheet software, such as Microsoft Excel, is a powerful tool used for data analysis, calculation, organization, and visualization. It allows users to create electronic worksheets consisting of rows and columns, where data can be entered, manipulated, and analyzed. Here are key components and concepts of spreadsheet software:

1. Cells, Rows, and Columns : A spreadsheet is organized into cells, which are the individual boxes where data can be entered. Cells are arranged in rows (horizontal) and columns (vertical). Each cell is identified by a unique combination of its column letter and row number (e.g., A1, B2).

2. Data Entry and Formatting : Users can enter various types of data into cells, including numbers, text, dates, and formulas. Spreadsheet software provides formatting options to customize the appearance of data, such as font styles, colors, alignment, and cell borders.

3. Formulas and Functions : Formulas are mathematical expressions used to perform calculations on data in a spreadsheet. Functions are predefined formulas that perform specific tasks, such as SUM (to add numbers), AVERAGE (to calculate the average), and IF (to perform conditional logic). Functions can be used to analyze data, perform complex calculations, and automate repetitive tasks.

4. Data Analysis and Manipulation : Spreadsheet software provides tools for data analysis and manipulation, such as sorting, filtering, and pivot tables. Users can sort data alphabetically or numerically, filter data to display specific records, and create pivot tables to summarize and analyze large datasets.

5. Charts and Graphs : Spreadsheet software allows users to create charts and graphs to visualize data and trends. Users can choose from various chart types, such as bar charts, line charts, pie charts, and scatter plots, and customize the appearance of charts with different colors, labels, and formatting options.

6. Data Validation : Data validation features allow users to control the type and format of data entered into cells. Users can define rules and criteria to validate data, such as restricting input to certain values, dates, or number ranges, and display error messages for invalid entries.

7. Data Import and Export : Spreadsheet software supports importing data from external sources, such as databases, text files, and web pages, allowing users to analyze data from multiple sources in one place. Users can also export data from spreadsheets to other formats for sharing or further analysis.

8. Collaboration and Sharing : Spreadsheet software facilitates collaboration among multiple users by allowing them to work on the same spreadsheet simultaneously. Users can share spreadsheets with others via email, cloud storage, or collaboration platforms, and track changes made by different users.

9. Automation and Macros : Spreadsheet software offers automation features, such as macros and scripting, to streamline repetitive tasks and increase productivity. Users

can record macros to automate sequences of actions or write scripts using programming languages like Visual Basic for Applications (VBA) to create custom functions and automate complex tasks.

10. Data Security and Protection : Spreadsheet software includes features for data security and protection, such as password protection, encryption, and access controls. Users can restrict access to sensitive data, encrypt files to prevent unauthorized access, and implement security measures to protect against data breaches and unauthorized changes.

Spreadsheet software is a versatile tool used in various industries and disciplines, including finance, accounting, engineering, science, education, and business. It provides users with the flexibility to organize, analyze, and visualize data effectively, making it an essential tool for data management and decision-making in today's digital age.

Ideas for Study Material/Resources:
Books: "Excel 2019 Bible" by Michael Alexander and Richard Kusleika, "Excel Formulas & Functions For Dummies" by Ken Bluttman and Peter G. Aitken, "Financial Modeling in Excel For Dummies" by Danielle Stein Fairhurst.
Online Courses: Platforms like LinkedIn Learning, Udemy, and Coursera offer a wide range of Excel courses, from beginner to advanced levels, covering topics like formulas, data analysis, macros, and dashboard creation.
Tutorials and Guides: Websites like Excel Easy, Chandoo.org, and Exceljet provide free tutorials, guides, and templates for learning Excel functions, formulas, shortcuts, and tips.

Ideas for Activity:
Assign practical Excel exercises and projects, such as creating budgets, analyzing sales data, building financial models, or designing interactive dashboards, to reinforce Excel skills and demonstrate real-world applications.
Organize Excel workshops or training sessions where participants collaborate on solving Excel challenges, sharing tips and tricks, and exploring advanced features together.

Some Training Ideas for Facilitation:
Start with an introduction to Excel's interface, including navigating worksheets, entering data, formatting cells, and managing workbooks.
Teach fundamental Excel functions and formulas, such as SUM, VLOOKUP, IF statements, and PivotTables, and demonstrate how to use them for data manipulation, analysis, and reporting.
Provide guidance on advanced Excel features, including conditional formatting, data validation, goal seeking, scenario analysis, and automation using macros and VBA (Visual Basic for Applications).

Did You Know?
Excel offers over 400 built-in functions, ranging from basic arithmetic operations to advanced statistical, financial, and engineering calculations.

Ideas for Presentation:
Create a PowerPoint presentation or e-book covering key Excel concepts, functions, and techniques. Include step-by-step tutorials, screenshots, and examples to illustrate Excel features and best practices effectively.

Training Video Guide:
Develop video tutorials or Excel training videos demonstrating how to use Excel functions, formulas, and features. Record screen demonstrations, walkthroughs, and tutorials to help learners visualize and understand Excel concepts and workflows more effectively.

Skill 61: Word Processing Software (e.g., Word)

Importance:
Proficiency in word processing software, such as Microsoft Word, is essential for creating, editing, formatting, and sharing documents in various professional and academic settings. Word processing skills are valuable for writing reports, letters, resumes, and other documents with clarity, consistency, and professionalism.

Concept:
Word processing software enables users to compose text, format documents, insert images and graphics, and collaborate with others on writing projects. Proficiency in Word involves mastering its features, such as styles, formatting tools, templates, and collaboration functionalities.

Takeaway: Guide for Students and Professionals
By mastering word processing software skills, individuals can enhance their written communication, streamline document creation and editing processes, and produce polished and professional-looking documents. Word processing proficiency is essential for professionals across industries, including business, education, and administration. Word processing software, such as Microsoft Word, is a versatile tool used for creating, editing, formatting, and sharing text-based documents. It provides a range of features and functionalities to facilitate document creation and editing tasks. Here are key components and concepts of word processing software:

1.   Document Creation : Word processing software allows users to create new documents from scratch or use pre-designed templates for common document types, such as letters, resumes, reports, and flyers. Users can start with a blank document or choose from a variety of templates to get started quickly.

2. Text Entry and Formatting : Users can enter and format text in a document using a range of formatting options, such as font styles, sizes, colors, and alignment. Word processing software provides tools for applying formatting styles, bulleted or numbered lists, indents, margins, and line spacing to enhance the appearance of text.

3. Editing and Proofreading : Word processing software includes editing and proofreading tools to help users review and refine their documents. Users can correct spelling and grammar errors using built-in spelling and grammar checkers, as well as track changes, add comments, and collaborate with others on document revisions.

4. Formatting Styles and Themes : Word processing software offers built-in formatting styles and themes to apply consistent formatting throughout a document. Users can choose from a variety of predefined styles for headings, titles, paragraphs, and other text elements, or create custom styles to suit their specific needs.

5. Page Layout and Design : Word processing software allows users to control the layout and design of their documents, including page size, orientation, margins, and page breaks. Users can insert headers, footers, page numbers, and other design elements to enhance the appearance and readability of their documents.

6. Graphics and Multimedia Integration : Word processing software supports the integration of graphics, images, charts, and multimedia elements into documents. Users can insert and resize images, create and modify charts and graphs, and embed audio or video files to add visual interest and enhance the presentation of information.

7. Tables and Spreadsheets : Word processing software includes tools for creating and formatting tables and spreadsheets within documents. Users can insert tables to organize data into rows and columns, apply formatting to table elements, and perform calculations using built-in formulas and functions.

8. Document Collaboration and Sharing : Word processing software facilitates collaboration among multiple users by allowing them to work on the same document simultaneously. Users can share documents with others via email, cloud storage, or collaboration platforms, and track changes made by different users.

9. Document Security and Protection : Word processing software includes features for document security and protection, such as password protection, encryption, and access controls. Users can restrict access to sensitive documents, encrypt files to prevent unauthorized access, and implement security measures to protect against data breaches.

10. Document Export and Printing : Word processing software supports exporting documents to various file formats for sharing or archiving purposes, such as PDF, HTML, or plain text. Users can also print documents directly from the software, choosing from a range of printing options and settings to produce high-quality printed copies.

Word processing software is widely used in various industries and disciplines, including business, education, government, and publishing. It provides users with the tools and functionalities needed to create professional-looking documents, communicate effectively, and collaborate with others on document projects.

Ideas for Study Material/Resources:
Books: "Microsoft Word 2019 Step by Step" by Joan Lambert and Curtis Frye, "Word For Dummies" by Dan Gookin, "The Only Word 2019 Book You'll Ever Need" by Sherry Kinkoph Gunter.
Online Courses: Platforms like LinkedIn Learning, Udemy, and Coursera offer comprehensive Word courses covering topics like document formatting, styles, templates, mail merge, and collaboration features.
Tutorials and Guides: Websites like Microsoft Office support, GCF LearnFree, and Word Tips provide free tutorials, guides, and templates for learning Word basics and advanced features.

Ideas for Activity:
Assign document creation and formatting tasks, such as writing reports, letters, resumes, or proposals, to practice Word skills and demonstrate proficiency in document layout, formatting, and design.
Organize collaborative writing projects or peer editing workshops where participants collaborate on creating, reviewing, and editing documents using Word's collaboration features and track changes.

Some Training Ideas for Facilitation:
Start with an overview of Word's interface, including the Ribbon, Quick Access Toolbar, and Navigation Pane, and introduce basic document creation and editing functionalities.
Teach document formatting techniques, including styles, fonts, paragraph formatting, headers and footers, page layout, and section breaks, to create professional-looking documents efficiently.
Provide guidance on advanced Word features, such as mail merge, tables of contents, footnotes and endnotes, cross-references, and document automation using macros.

Did You Know?
Microsoft Word was first released in 1983 and has since become one of the most widely used word processing software applications worldwide.

Ideas for Presentation:
Create a PowerPoint presentation or e-book covering key Word concepts, features, and techniques. Include step-by-step tutorials, screenshots, and examples to illustrate Word functionalities and best practices effectively.

Training Video Guide:
Develop video tutorials or Word training videos demonstrating how to use Word's features and functions. Record screen demonstrations, walkthroughs, and tutorials to help learners visualize and understand Word workflows and techniques more effectively.

Skill 62: ERP (Enterprise Resource Planning) Systems

Importance:
Enterprise Resource Planning (ERP) systems are essential for integrating and managing core business processes, including finance, human resources, supply chain management, and customer relationship management. Proficiency in ERP systems allows organizations to streamline operations, improve efficiency, and make data-driven decisions.

Concept:
ERP systems are software platforms that centralize and automate various business functions, such as accounting, procurement, inventory management, and order processing, into a single integrated system. Proficiency in ERP involves understanding system modules, data structures, workflows, and reporting capabilities.

Takeaway: Guide for Students and Professionals
By mastering ERP system skills, individuals can effectively navigate and utilize ERP software to perform tasks like data entry, report generation, process automation, and system customization. ERP proficiency is valuable for professionals working in business analysis, consulting, IT, and operations roles.

Enterprise Resource Planning (ERP) systems are integrated software solutions used by organizations to manage and streamline their business processes, operations, and resources across various departments and functions. ERP systems provide a centralized platform for managing core business activities, including finance, human resources, supply chain management, inventory, manufacturing, sales, and customer relationship management (CRM). Here are key components and concepts of ERP systems:

1. Integration : ERP systems integrate data and processes from different departments and functions within an organization into a unified system. This integration allows for real-time visibility and access to critical business information across the entire organization, enabling better decision-making and collaboration.

2. Modules : ERP systems consist of multiple modules or applications that address specific business functions and processes. Common ERP modules include finance and accounting, human resources management (HRM), supply chain management (SCM), inventory management, manufacturing, sales and distribution, and CRM.

3. Core Functions : ERP systems provide core functions to support key business processes and operations. These functions may include financial management (e.g., general ledger, accounts payable, accounts receivable, budgeting), procurement and purchasing, inventory control, production planning, order management, and customer service.

4. Data Management : ERP systems store and manage large volumes of data related to business transactions, processes, and activities. They provide tools and

functionalities for data entry, storage, retrieval, manipulation, and analysis, ensuring data accuracy, consistency, and integrity across the organization.

5. Workflow Automation : ERP systems automate and streamline business processes and workflows by eliminating manual tasks, reducing paperwork, and improving efficiency. They offer workflow automation features such as automated notifications, approvals, reminders, and escalations to optimize process execution and minimize delays.

6. Reporting and Analytics : ERP systems include reporting and analytics tools to help organizations monitor and analyze their business performance. Users can generate standard and custom reports, dashboards, and key performance indicators (KPIs) to gain insights into key metrics, trends, and areas for improvement.

7. Customization and Configuration : ERP systems are highly customizable and configurable to meet the unique needs and requirements of different organizations. They allow users to customize workflows, forms, reports, and interfaces, as well as configure settings, permissions, and security policies to align with organizational processes and policies.

8. Scalability : ERP systems are scalable and capable of supporting organizations of all sizes, from small businesses to large enterprises. They can scale up to accommodate growth and expansion, as well as scale down to meet the needs of smaller organizations or specific business units.

9. Cloud-Based Deployment : Many ERP systems offer cloud-based deployment options, allowing organizations to access and use the software over the internet as a service (SaaS). Cloud-based ERP solutions offer benefits such as scalability, flexibility, accessibility, and lower upfront costs compared to traditional on-premises deployments.

10. Integration with Third-Party Systems : ERP systems can integrate with third-party software applications, systems, and services to extend functionality, enhance interoperability, and streamline business processes. Integration options may include APIs (Application Programming Interfaces), connectors, middleware, and data synchronization tools.

By implementing an ERP system, organizations can improve operational efficiency, optimize resource utilization, enhance decision-making, and achieve better business outcomes. ERP systems provide a comprehensive and centralized solution for managing and coordinating all aspects of an organization's operations, helping to drive growth, innovation, and competitive advantage in today's dynamic business environment.

Ideas for Study Material/Resources:
Books: "ERP: Tools, Techniques, and Applications for Integrating the Supply Chain" by Carol A. Ptak and Eli Schragenheim, "Implementing SAP ERP Sales & Distribution" by Glynn C. Williams, "Microsoft Dynamics 365 For Dummies" by Renato Bellu.

Online Courses: Platforms like Udemy, Coursera, and LinkedIn Learning offer courses on ERP systems, including SAP, Oracle, Microsoft Dynamics, and NetSuite, covering topics like implementation, configuration, and user training.

Vendor Documentation: ERP vendors provide online documentation, user guides, tutorials, and training materials for their specific ERP systems, accessible through their official websites or customer portals.

Ideas for Activity:
Conduct ERP system simulations or case studies where participants work through real-life business scenarios, such as order processing, inventory management, or financial reporting, using ERP software.

Organize hands-on workshops or training sessions where participants practice navigating ERP system interfaces, performing common tasks, and generating reports using sample data sets.

Some Training Ideas for Facilitation:
Start by introducing participants to the purpose and functions of ERP systems and their role in integrating business processes and data across departments and functions.

Provide an overview of key ERP modules, such as finance, sales, procurement, inventory, and production, and explain how they interact within the ERP system architecture.

Demonstrate how to perform common tasks in the ERP system, including data entry, transaction processing, report generation, and system configuration, and provide guidance on best practices and system shortcuts.

Did You Know?
ERP systems originated in the manufacturing industry in the 1960s and have since evolved to encompass various industries and business functions, becoming a cornerstone of modern business operations.

Ideas for Presentation:
Create a PowerPoint presentation or e-book summarizing key ERP concepts, modules, and functionalities. Include screenshots, diagrams, and examples to illustrate ERP workflows, data flows, and system architecture effectively.

Training Video Guide:
Develop video tutorials or ERP training videos demonstrating how to navigate and use ERP system interfaces, perform common tasks, and generate reports. Record screen demonstrations and walkthroughs to help learners understand ERP system functionalities and workflows visually.

Skill 63: Statistical Analysis Software (e.g., SPSS, SAS)

Importance:
Proficiency in statistical analysis software is crucial for conducting data analysis, hypothesis testing, and statistical modeling in various fields, including research,

academia, healthcare, finance, and marketing. Statistical analysis software enables researchers and analysts to derive insights from data, make informed decisions, and solve complex problems.

Concept:
Statistical analysis software provides tools and techniques for summarizing, visualizing, and interpreting data, as well as conducting statistical tests and modeling relationships between variables. Proficiency in statistical analysis involves understanding statistical concepts, software features, data manipulation, and interpretation of results.

Takeaway: Guide for Students and Professionals
By mastering statistical analysis software skills, individuals can perform data analysis tasks such as descriptive statistics, hypothesis testing, regression analysis, and survival analysis. Statistical analysis proficiency is valuable for professionals in fields such as research, data science, biostatistics, and market research.
Statistical Analysis Software (SAS) is a powerful tool used by researchers, statisticians, and data analysts to analyze, interpret, and visualize data. It provides a wide range of statistical techniques and methods for exploring relationships, making predictions, and drawing conclusions from data. Here are key components and concepts of statistical analysis software:

1. Data Import and Preparation : Statistical analysis software allows users to import data from various sources, such as spreadsheets, databases, and text files. Users can clean, preprocess, and transform data to prepare it for analysis, including data cleaning, missing value imputation, variable transformation, and data aggregation.

2. Descriptive Statistics : SAS provides tools for computing descriptive statistics, such as measures of central tendency (mean, median, mode), measures of dispersion (standard deviation, variance, range), and measures of distribution (skewness, kurtosis). Descriptive statistics summarize and describe the characteristics of a dataset, providing insights into its distribution and variability.

3. Inferential Statistics : SAS offers a wide range of inferential statistical techniques for making inferences and testing hypotheses about population parameters based on sample data. These techniques include hypothesis testing, confidence intervals, analysis of variance (ANOVA), regression analysis, chi-square tests, and nonparametric tests.

4. Regression Analysis : Regression analysis is a statistical technique used to model and analyze the relationship between one or more independent variables (predictors) and a dependent variable (outcome). SAS provides various regression models, such as linear regression, logistic regression, multiple regression, and generalized linear models (GLMs), for predicting and understanding the relationship between variables.

5. Data Visualization : SAS offers tools for visualizing data and results using charts, graphs, and plots. Users can create histograms, scatter plots, bar charts, line charts,

box plots, and other visualizations to explore patterns, trends, and relationships in the data and communicate findings effectively.

6. Time Series Analysis : Time series analysis is a statistical technique used to analyze time-ordered data and identify patterns, trends, and seasonality. SAS provides tools for time series forecasting, decomposition, smoothing, and autocorrelation analysis to analyze and model time series data.

7. Cluster Analysis : Cluster analysis is a statistical technique used to identify natural groupings or clusters within a dataset based on similarities or dissimilarities between observations. SAS offers algorithms for hierarchical clustering, k-means clustering, and other clustering methods to partition data into meaningful clusters and explore patterns within the data.

8. Factor Analysis and Dimensionality Reduction : Factor analysis is a statistical technique used to identify underlying factors or latent variables that explain the correlations between observed variables. SAS provides tools for exploratory factor analysis (EFA), confirmatory factor analysis (CFA), and principal component analysis (PCA) to reduce the dimensionality of data and identify underlying structures.

9. Survival Analysis : Survival analysis is a statistical technique used to analyze time-to-event data, such as time until failure, recurrence, or death. SAS provides tools for survival analysis, including Kaplan-Meier estimation, Cox proportional hazards regression, and parametric survival models, to analyze and model survival data.

10. Modeling and Prediction : SAS offers advanced modeling and prediction techniques for building predictive models and making forecasts based on historical data. Users can build predictive models using machine learning algorithms, such as decision trees, random forests, neural networks, support vector machines (SVM), and ensemble methods, to predict outcomes, classify observations, and identify patterns in the data.

By leveraging the capabilities of statistical analysis software like SAS, users can gain valuable insights from data, make informed decisions, and solve complex problems in a wide range of fields, including business, healthcare, finance, marketing, and research. Statistical analysis software plays a crucial role in data-driven decision-making, enabling organizations to extract actionable insights and drive innovation and growth.

Ideas for Study Material/Resources:
Books: "SPSS Survival Manual" by Julie Pallant, "Statistics for People Who (Think They) Hate Statistics" by Neil J. Salkind, "SAS Programming for R Users" by Cody H. Moug and Michael A. Smith.
Online Courses: Platforms like Coursera, Udemy, and LinkedIn Learning offer courses on statistical analysis software, covering topics such as data analysis, regression, ANOVA, and multivariate analysis using software like SPSS, SAS, R, and Python.

Software Documentation: Statistical analysis software vendors provide online documentation, tutorials, and user guides for their software products, accessible through their official websites or customer support portals.

Ideas for Activity:
Assign data analysis projects or case studies where participants use statistical analysis software to analyze real-world datasets, perform statistical tests, and interpret results. Organize hands-on workshops or training sessions where participants practice using statistical analysis software to perform common data analysis tasks, such as data cleaning, variable transformation, and model building.

Some Training Ideas for Facilitation:
Start by introducing participants to the purpose and capabilities of statistical analysis software and their role in data analysis and hypothesis testing.
Provide an overview of key statistical techniques and procedures supported by the software, such as descriptive statistics, inferential statistics, regression analysis, and factor analysis.
Demonstrate how to perform common data analysis tasks in the software, including data import, variable manipulation, statistical tests, model estimation, and result interpretation, and provide guidance on best practices and troubleshooting.

Did You Know?
SPSS (Statistical Package for the Social Sciences) was originally developed in the late 1960s by Norman H. Nie, C. Hadlai "Tex" Hull, and Dale H. Bent, and is widely used in social science research.
SAS (Statistical Analysis System) was developed in the 1970s by Anthony James Barr and colleagues at North Carolina State University and is widely used in industries such as healthcare, finance, and pharmaceuticals.

Ideas for Presentation:
Create a PowerPoint presentation or e-book summarizing key statistical analysis concepts, techniques, and procedures supported by the software. Include screenshots, examples, and case studies to illustrate statistical analysis workflows and interpretation of results effectively.

Training Video Guide:
Develop video tutorials or statistical analysis software training videos demonstrating how to use the software interface, perform common data analysis tasks, and interpret statistical results. Record screen demonstrations, walkthroughs, and tutorials to help learners understand software functionalities and workflows visually.

Skill 64: Email Marketing Tools

Importance:
Email marketing tools are essential for businesses to create, automate, and optimize email campaigns for customer engagement, lead generation, and sales conversion.

Proficiency in email marketing tools allows marketers to reach target audiences effectively, track campaign performance, and personalize communication for better results.

Concept:
Email marketing tools provide features for creating email templates, managing subscriber lists, scheduling email campaigns, and tracking metrics such as open rates, click-through rates, and conversion rates. Proficiency in email marketing involves understanding tool functionalities, best practices for email design, and strategies for audience segmentation and targeting.

Takeaway: Guide for Students and Professionals
By mastering email marketing tools, individuals can create impactful email campaigns, nurture customer relationships, and drive business growth through effective communication and engagement. Email marketing proficiency is valuable for marketers, business owners, and professionals in sales and customer service roles.
Email marketing tools are software platforms designed to facilitate the creation, management, and analysis of email marketing campaigns. These tools provide features and functionalities to help businesses and marketers effectively engage with their subscribers, build relationships, and drive conversions through email communication. Here are key components and concepts of email marketing tools:

1. Email Campaign Creation : Email marketing tools allow users to create and design professional-looking email campaigns using customizable templates, drag-and-drop editors, and content blocks. Users can add text, images, videos, buttons, and links to create engaging email content that resonates with their audience.

2. Contact Management : Email marketing tools provide contact management features to organize and manage subscriber lists, segments, and contact data. Users can import, export, and segment contacts based on various criteria, such as demographics, behavior, interests, and engagement history.

3. List Growth and Lead Capture : Email marketing tools offer tools and integrations to grow subscriber lists and capture leads through various channels, such as website sign-up forms, landing pages, pop-ups, and social media integrations. Users can create and customize opt-in forms to capture visitor information and grow their email list.

4. Personalization and Segmentation : Email marketing tools enable users to personalize email content and tailor messages to specific segments of their audience. Users can personalize subject lines, greetings, and content based on subscriber data, preferences, and behaviors to increase engagement and relevance.

5. Automation and Workflows : Email marketing tools support automation and workflow capabilities to streamline repetitive tasks, nurture leads, and deliver personalized email experiences at scale. Users can set up automated email sequences, drip campaigns, and triggered emails based on predefined triggers, events, or subscriber actions.

6. A/B Testing : Email marketing tools include A/B testing (split testing) features to experiment with different elements of email campaigns and optimize performance. Users can test variations of subject lines, email content, calls-to-action, and sending times to identify what resonates best with their audience and improve campaign results.

7. Email Scheduling and Delivery : Email marketing tools allow users to schedule and send emails at optimal times to maximize engagement and deliverability. Users can schedule one-time or recurring campaigns, set up time-based triggers, and use send-time optimization features to deliver emails when subscribers are most likely to engage.

8. Analytics and Reporting : Email marketing tools provide analytics and reporting dashboards to track and measure the performance of email campaigns. Users can monitor key metrics such as open rates, click-through rates, conversion rates, bounce rates, and unsubscribe rates to assess campaign effectiveness and identify areas for improvement.

9. Compliance and Deliverability : Email marketing tools ensure compliance with email regulations and standards, such as CAN-SPAM and GDPR, to protect sender reputation and ensure email deliverability. They provide features for managing unsubscribe requests, handling bounces, and maintaining email compliance to minimize the risk of spam complaints and deliver emails to subscribers' inboxes.

10. Integration and Ecosystem : Email marketing tools integrate with other marketing platforms, CRM systems, and third-party applications to streamline workflows, synchronize data, and enhance functionality. Users can integrate email marketing tools with customer databases, e-commerce platforms, social media channels, and analytics tools to create seamless multichannel marketing campaigns.

By leveraging the capabilities of email marketing tools, businesses and marketers can create targeted, personalized, and data-driven email campaigns that engage subscribers, drive conversions, and achieve their marketing goals effectively. Email marketing tools play a crucial role in building and nurturing customer relationships, driving revenue, and maximizing the ROI of email marketing efforts.

Ideas for Study Material/Resources:
Books: "Email Marketing Rules: Checklists, Frameworks, and 150 Best Practices for Business Success" by Chad S. White, "Email Persuasion: Captivate and Engage Your Audience, Build Authority and Generate More Sales With Email Marketing" by Ian Brodie, "The Complete Guide to B2B Email Marketing" by Juanita McDowell.
Online Courses: Platforms like Udemy, Coursera, and HubSpot Academy offer courses on email marketing, covering topics such as email campaign management, list building, segmentation, and email automation using tools like Mailchimp, Constant Contact, and HubSpot.
Blogs and Guides: Websites like HubSpot, Mailchimp, and Campaign Monitor provide comprehensive guides, tutorials, and best practices for email marketing, covering topics such as email design, deliverability, A/B testing, and GDPR compliance.

Ideas for Activity:
Assign email campaign creation projects where participants use email marketing tools to design and launch email campaigns targeting specific audience segments or marketing objectives.
Organize A/B testing experiments where participants create variations of email campaigns using different subject lines, content, or calls to action, and analyze performance metrics to identify effective strategies.

Some Training Ideas for Facilitation:
Start by introducing participants to the purpose and benefits of email marketing tools and their role in creating, managing, and analyzing email campaigns.
Provide an overview of key features and functionalities offered by email marketing tools, such as email templates, list segmentation, automation workflows, and analytics dashboards.
Demonstrate how to use email marketing tools to create and send email campaigns, manage subscriber lists, segment audiences, set up automation workflows, and analyze campaign performance metrics.

Did You Know?
Email marketing has one of the highest ROI (Return on Investment) among digital marketing channels, with an average ROI of $42 for every $1 spent, according to a study by Litmus.
Personalized email campaigns generate six times higher transaction rates than non-personalized campaigns, according to Experian.

Ideas for Presentation:
Create a PowerPoint presentation or e-book summarizing key email marketing concepts, strategies, and best practices. Include examples, case studies, and screenshots of email marketing tools to illustrate effective email campaign design and optimization.

Training Video Guide:
Develop video tutorials or email marketing tool training videos demonstrating how to use popular email marketing tools to create and manage email campaigns. Record screen demonstrations, walkthroughs, and tutorials to help learners understand tool functionalities and workflows visually.

Skill 65: Content/Learning Management Systems (CMS/LMS)

Importance:
Content and Learning Management Systems (CMS/LMS) are crucial for organizing, delivering, and managing educational content and training materials. Proficiency in CMS/LMS enables educators, trainers, and organizations to create engaging learning experiences, track learner progress, and administer assessments efficiently.

Concept:
CMS/LMS platforms provide features for creating, organizing, and delivering multimedia content, such as courses, quizzes, assignments, and discussions. Proficiency in CMS/LMS involves understanding platform functionalities, course design principles, learner engagement strategies, and assessment methods.

Takeaway: Guide for Students and Professionals
By mastering CMS/LMS skills, individuals can design and deliver effective online courses, training programs, and educational materials for diverse audiences. CMS/LMS proficiency is valuable for educators, instructional designers, trainers, and HR professionals involved in employee training and development.
Content Management Systems (CMS) and Learning Management Systems (LMS) are software platforms designed to create, manage, deliver, and track digital content and learning materials. While CMS focuses on content creation and management for websites and online platforms, LMS specifically caters to e-learning and training initiatives. Here are key components and concepts of CMS and LMS:

1. Content Creation and Authoring : CMS and LMS platforms provide tools for creating and authoring digital content, including text, images, videos, presentations, quizzes, assessments, and interactive multimedia. Users can create content using built-in editors, templates, and multimedia libraries, or import existing content from external sources.

2. Content Management and Organization : CMS and LMS platforms offer content management features to organize and categorize digital assets, resources, and learning materials. Users can create hierarchies, taxonomies, and folders to structure content logically, and tag content with metadata for easy searching and retrieval.

3. User Management and Authentication : CMS and LMS platforms support user management and authentication features to control access to digital content and learning resources. Users can create user accounts, assign roles and permissions, and authenticate users through login credentials, single sign-on (SSO), or integration with identity management systems.

4. Content Delivery and Distribution : CMS and LMS platforms enable users to deliver digital content and learning materials to target audiences through various channels and devices. Content can be delivered via web browsers, mobile apps, email, social media, or integration with other platforms and systems.

5. Learning Pathways and Curriculum : LMS platforms offer features for creating learning pathways, courses, and curriculum to guide learners through structured learning experiences. Users can create course modules, lessons, assignments, and assessments, and sequence them into learning paths or curriculum tracks.

6. Assessment and Evaluation : LMS platforms include assessment and evaluation tools to measure learner progress, performance, and achievement. Users can create quizzes, tests, surveys, and assignments to assess learner knowledge, skills, and competencies, and track learner responses and scores.

7. Progress Tracking and Reporting : CMS and LMS platforms provide progress tracking and reporting features to monitor learner activity, engagement, and performance. Users can track learner progress through course completion metrics, activity logs, and performance dashboards, and generate reports to analyze learning outcomes and trends.

8. Collaboration and Interaction : CMS and LMS platforms facilitate collaboration and interaction among learners, instructors, and peers through discussion forums, chat rooms, messaging, and collaboration tools. Users can engage in asynchronous and synchronous communication, share ideas, ask questions, and collaborate on projects and assignments.

9. Integration and Interoperability : CMS and LMS platforms integrate with other systems, tools, and services to enhance functionality, streamline workflows, and extend capabilities. Users can integrate CMS and LMS platforms with learning content repositories, assessment tools, video conferencing systems, analytics platforms, and external learning resources.

10. Accessibility and Compliance : CMS and LMS platforms adhere to accessibility standards and compliance requirements to ensure that digital content and learning materials are accessible to all learners, including those with disabilities. They provide features for creating accessible content, such as alternative text for images, keyboard navigation, and screen reader compatibility.

By leveraging the capabilities of CMS and LMS platforms, organizations, educational institutions, and training providers can create engaging, interactive, and personalized learning experiences, deliver high-quality digital content and training materials, and track learner progress and performance effectively. CMS and LMS platforms play a crucial role in enabling online learning, training, and professional development initiatives, empowering learners to acquire knowledge, skills, and competencies in today's digital age.

Ideas for Study Material/Resources:
Books: "E-Learning and the Science of Instruction: Proven Guidelines for Consumers and Designers of Multimedia Learning" by Ruth C. Clark and Richard E. Mayer, "Learning Management Systems and Instructional Design: Best Practices in Online Education" by Linda L. Baer and Peter Shea, "Teaching Online: A Practical Guide" by Susan Ko and Steve Rossen.
Online Courses: Platforms like Coursera, Udemy, and LinkedIn Learning offer courses on instructional design, e-learning development, and CMS/LMS platforms such as Moodle, Canvas, and Blackboard.
Documentation and Tutorials: CMS/LMS vendors provide online documentation, tutorials, and user guides for their platforms, covering topics such as course creation, user management, assessments, and analytics.

Ideas for Activity:
Assign course creation projects where participants use CMS/LMS platforms to design and develop online courses, including lesson planning, content creation, multimedia integration, and assessment design.
Organize hands-on workshops or training sessions where participants explore CMS/LMS platforms, create sample courses, and practice administering assessments and tracking learner progress.

Some Training Ideas for Facilitation:
Start by introducing participants to the purpose and features of CMS/LMS platforms and their role in online education and training delivery.
Provide an overview of key functionalities offered by CMS/LMS platforms, such as course creation, content management, user enrollment, discussion forums, and assessment tools.
Demonstrate how to use CMS/LMS platforms to create and manage online courses, upload multimedia content, design assessments, facilitate discussions, and monitor learner progress and engagement.

Did You Know?
Moodle, an open-source CMS/LMS platform, is used by millions of educators and organizations worldwide to create and deliver online courses.
Canvas, another popular CMS/LMS platform, is known for its user-friendly interface, mobile compatibility, and extensive integration capabilities with third-party tools and services.

Ideas for Presentation:
Create a PowerPoint presentation or e-book summarizing key CMS/LMS concepts, features, and best practices for course creation and delivery. Include screenshots, examples, and case studies to illustrate effective use of CMS/LMS platforms.

Training Video Guide:
Develop video tutorials or CMS/LMS platform training videos demonstrating how to use popular CMS/LMS platforms to create and manage online courses. Record screen demonstrations, walkthroughs, and tutorials to help learners navigate platform interfaces and workflows effectively.

Skill 66: Video Conferencing Tools (e.g., Zoom, Microsoft Teams)

Importance:
Video conferencing tools are essential for facilitating remote communication, collaboration, and virtual meetings among individuals and teams. Proficiency in video conferencing tools enables participants to connect, communicate, and collaborate effectively, regardless of geographical location.

Concept:
Video conferencing tools provide features for hosting virtual meetings, webinars, and online presentations, including video and audio communication, screen sharing, chat messaging, and recording capabilities. Proficiency in video conferencing involves understanding tool functionalities, meeting etiquette, and troubleshooting common issues.

Takeaway: Guide for Students and Professionals
By mastering video conferencing tools, individuals can host and participate in virtual meetings, webinars, and online events with confidence and professionalism. Video conferencing proficiency is valuable for remote workers, business professionals, educators, and anyone involved in virtual collaboration.
Video conferencing tools are software platforms designed to facilitate virtual meetings, conferences, and collaboration sessions through video and audio communication. These tools provide features and functionalities to connect remote participants, share content, and collaborate in real-time, enhancing communication and productivity. Here are key components and concepts of video conferencing tools:

1. Video and Audio Communication : Video conferencing tools enable participants to communicate with each other through live video and audio streams. Users can join virtual meetings from any location using webcams, microphones, and speakers or headsets, and engage in face-to-face conversations in real-time.

2. Meeting Scheduling and Invitations : Video conferencing tools offer features for scheduling and organizing meetings, including calendar integration, meeting invitations, and RSVP tracking. Users can schedule one-time or recurring meetings, set meeting agendas, and send invitations to participants via email or calendar invites.

3. Meeting Hosting and Moderation : Video conferencing tools allow users to host and moderate virtual meetings, controlling meeting settings, participants, and permissions. Hosts can start and end meetings, manage participant access, mute/unmute participants, and control screen sharing and presentation capabilities.

4. Screen Sharing and Content Sharing : Video conferencing tools support screen sharing and content sharing features to facilitate presentations, demonstrations, and collaboration. Users can share their screens, desktops, or specific applications with other participants, as well as share files, documents, presentations, and multimedia content in real-time.

5. Chat and Messaging : Video conferencing tools include chat and messaging features to facilitate text-based communication among participants during meetings. Users can send messages, chat privately with individuals or groups, share links and files, and collaborate through text chat alongside video and audio communication.

6. Virtual Backgrounds and Effects : Video conferencing tools offer virtual background and effects features to enhance the appearance and engagement of participants during meetings. Users can apply virtual backgrounds, blur backgrounds, or use custom backgrounds to maintain privacy or add visual interest to their video feeds.

7. Recording and Playback : Video conferencing tools allow users to record meetings and sessions for later playback, review, or sharing. Hosts or administrators can record meetings locally or in the cloud, capture audio, video, and screen sharing, and share recordings with participants or distribute them for training or documentation purposes.

8. Participant Management and Controls : Video conferencing tools provide controls and options for managing participants and interactions during meetings. Hosts can admit participants from waiting rooms, manage attendee permissions, assign roles and privileges, and enforce meeting policies and guidelines.

9. Security and Privacy : Video conferencing tools prioritize security and privacy features to protect meeting data, communications, and participant information. They offer encryption, authentication, access controls, and security settings to prevent unauthorized access, ensure data confidentiality, and comply with privacy regulations.

10. Integration and Collaboration : Video conferencing tools integrate with other collaboration tools, productivity suites, and business applications to enhance functionality and streamline workflows. Users can integrate video conferencing tools with calendar apps, email clients, project management platforms, and messaging tools to facilitate seamless communication and collaboration.

By leveraging the capabilities of video conferencing tools, organizations, teams, and individuals can connect, collaborate, and communicate effectively in virtual environments, regardless of geographical locations or time zones. Video conferencing tools play a crucial role in enabling remote work, virtual meetings, distance learning, and online collaboration, fostering productivity, engagement, and connectivity in today's digital workplace.

Ideas for Study Material/Resources:
Documentation and Tutorials: Video conferencing tool providers offer online documentation, tutorials, and user guides for their platforms, covering topics such as meeting setup, participant management, screen sharing, and recording.
Online Courses: Platforms like LinkedIn Learning, Udemy, and Coursera offer courses on remote collaboration, virtual meetings, and specific video conferencing tools such as Zoom and Microsoft Teams.
Webinars and Workshops: Many organizations and training providers offer webinars and workshops on best practices for virtual meetings, effective communication, and maximizing productivity with video conferencing tools.

Ideas for Activity:
Conduct virtual meetings or webinars where participants practice using video conferencing tools to host and participate in online meetings, share screens, engage in discussions, and collaborate on documents.
Organize breakout sessions or group activities where participants work together in virtual teams to solve problems, brainstorm ideas, or complete tasks using video conferencing tools.

Some Training Ideas for Facilitation:
Start by introducing participants to the purpose and benefits of video conferencing tools and their role in facilitating remote communication and collaboration.
Provide an overview of key features and functionalities offered by video conferencing tools, such as meeting scheduling, participant management, screen sharing, chat messaging, and recording.
Demonstrate how to host and participate in virtual meetings, manage meeting settings, share screens and documents, use chat messaging, and troubleshoot common issues with video conferencing tools.

Did You Know?
Zoom, founded in 2011, quickly became one of the most popular video conferencing platforms, known for its ease of use, reliability, and scalability.
Microsoft Teams, launched in 2017, is integrated with the Microsoft Office 365 suite and offers features such as chat, file sharing, and collaboration tools in addition to video conferencing.

Ideas for Presentation:
Create a PowerPoint presentation or e-book summarizing key video conferencing concepts, features, and best practices for hosting and participating in virtual meetings. Include tips, tricks, and etiquette guidelines for effective online communication and collaboration.

Training Video Guide:
Develop video tutorials or video conferencing tool training videos demonstrating how to use popular video conferencing platforms such as Zoom and Microsoft Teams. Record screen demonstrations, walkthroughs, and tutorials to help learners navigate platform interfaces and functionalities effectively.

Skill 67: Public Relations

Importance:
Public relations (PR) plays a vital role in shaping public perception, managing reputation, and building relationships with key stakeholders, including customers, media, investors, and the general public. Proficiency in PR enables individuals and organizations to effectively communicate their messages, manage crises, and maintain a positive public image.

Concept:
Public relations involves strategic communication efforts aimed at influencing public opinion, promoting positive relationships, and enhancing brand visibility and credibility. Proficiency in PR encompasses skills such as media relations, crisis communication, event planning, and content creation for various communication channels.

Takeaway: Guide for Students and Professionals
By mastering public relations skills, individuals can effectively manage public perception, enhance brand reputation, and cultivate positive relationships with stakeholders. PR proficiency is valuable for communication professionals, marketing specialists, business leaders, and anyone involved in managing public perception and reputation.

Public relations (PR) is a strategic communication discipline focused on building and maintaining mutually beneficial relationships between organizations and their target audiences, stakeholders, and the general public. PR professionals use various tactics and techniques to manage perceptions, shape public opinion, and enhance the reputation and image of organizations. Here are key components and concepts of public relations:

1. Media Relations : Media relations is a core component of PR, involving the management of relationships with journalists, reporters, editors, and media outlets. PR professionals pitch stories, press releases, and news angles to media contacts to secure coverage and visibility for their organizations or clients.

2. Press Releases and Media Kits : Press releases and media kits are tools used by PR professionals to disseminate news and information to the media and the public. Press releases provide concise summaries of newsworthy events, announcements, or developments, while media kits contain additional background information, images, and resources for journalists.

3. Crisis Communication : Crisis communication is a critical aspect of PR, involving the management of communication during emergencies, crises, or reputational threats. PR professionals develop crisis communication plans, protocols, and strategies to address issues, manage perceptions, and protect the reputation and credibility of organizations.

4. Corporate Communications : Corporate communications involves the development and dissemination of messages, information, and announcements related to an organization's activities, initiatives, and achievements. PR professionals handle corporate communications through various channels, including press releases, statements, speeches, and internal communications.

5. Publicity and Promotion : PR professionals generate publicity and promote organizations, products, services, or events through earned media coverage, influencer partnerships, sponsorships, and promotional campaigns. They leverage media opportunities, events, and initiatives to raise awareness, attract attention, and generate positive publicity.

6. Community Relations : Community relations involve engaging with and building relationships with local communities, stakeholders, and interest groups. PR professionals develop community outreach programs, sponsorships, and partnerships to support community initiatives, address social issues, and demonstrate corporate social responsibility.

7. Social Media and Digital PR : Social media and digital PR encompass the use of online platforms and digital channels to engage with audiences, disseminate information, and manage reputation. PR professionals leverage social media platforms, blogs, websites, and online forums to communicate messages, respond to feedback, and monitor online conversations.

8. Reputation Management : Reputation management involves monitoring, assessing, and shaping the reputation and perception of organizations among key stakeholders and the public. PR professionals use strategies and tactics to enhance positive perceptions, address negative sentiment, and manage online reputation through proactive communication and engagement.

9. Thought Leadership : Thought leadership involves positioning individuals or organizations as experts and thought leaders in their industry or field. PR professionals develop thought leadership strategies, content, and initiatives to showcase expertise, share insights, and contribute to industry conversations through articles, interviews, speaking engagements, and thought leadership platforms.

10. Measurement and Evaluation : Measurement and evaluation are essential components of PR, involving the assessment of PR efforts, outcomes, and impact. PR professionals use key performance indicators (KPIs), metrics, and analytics to measure media coverage, audience engagement, sentiment, and ROI, and evaluate the effectiveness of PR campaigns and activities.

By implementing effective PR strategies and tactics, organizations can enhance their reputation, credibility, and trustworthiness, build positive relationships with stakeholders, and achieve their communication and business objectives. PR plays a crucial role in shaping public perceptions, influencing behavior, and driving organizational success in today's competitive and interconnected world.

Ideas for Study Material/Resources:
Books: "The New Rules of Marketing and PR" by David Meerman Scott, "This Is PR: The Realities of Public Relations" by Doug Newsom, Judy VanSlyke Turk, and Dean Kruckeberg, "Trust Me, I'm Lying: Confessions of a Media Manipulator" by Ryan Holiday.
Online Courses: Platforms like Coursera, Udemy, and HubSpot Academy offer courses on public relations, covering topics such as media relations, crisis communication, social media PR, and PR strategy development.
Industry Publications: Websites like PRWeek, PR News, and Public Relations Society of America (PRSA) offer articles, case studies, and best practices on various aspects of public relations.

Ideas for Activity:
Assign PR campaign projects where participants develop strategic PR plans, including messaging, target audience identification, media outreach, and evaluation metrics.
Organize media training sessions or mock press conferences where participants practice handling media inquiries, interviews, and crisis scenarios.
Some Training Ideas for Facilitation:

Start by introducing participants to the role and importance of public relations in managing reputation, building relationships, and influencing public opinion.

Provide an overview of key PR strategies, tactics, and tools used in media relations, crisis communication, social media management, and event planning.

Demonstrate how to develop and execute PR campaigns, including setting objectives, identifying target audiences, crafting key messages, selecting communication channels, and evaluating campaign effectiveness.

Did You Know?

The term "public relations" was coined by Edward Bernays, often referred to as the "father of public relations," in the early 20th century.

PR professionals often use tools such as press releases, media pitches, press conferences, social media monitoring, and influencer outreach to manage communication and build relationships with various stakeholders.

Ideas for Presentation:

Create a PowerPoint presentation or e-book summarizing key public relations concepts, strategies, and best practices. Include case studies, examples, and practical tips for effective PR campaign development and execution.

Training Video Guide:

Develop video tutorials or PR training videos demonstrating key PR concepts, strategies, and techniques. Cover topics such as media relations, crisis communication, social media PR, and event planning. Use real-life examples and case studies to illustrate effective PR practices.

Soft Skill 68: Event Planning and Management

Importance:

Event planning and management involve organizing and executing events, ranging from corporate conferences and trade shows to weddings and charity fundraisers. Proficiency in event planning enables individuals to coordinate logistics, manage budgets, and ensure the success of various types of events.

Concept:

Event planning and management encompass a range of tasks, including venue selection, budgeting, vendor management, marketing and promotion, attendee registration, and on-site coordination. Proficiency in event planning requires strong organizational skills, attention to detail, creativity, and the ability to manage multiple tasks simultaneously.

Takeaway: Guide for Students and Professionals

By mastering event planning and management skills, individuals can successfully plan and execute memorable events that meet objectives, delight attendees, and achieve desired outcomes. Event planning proficiency is valuable for event planners, marketers, project managers, and anyone involved in organizing events.

Event planning and management is the process of organizing and executing events, gatherings, and experiences to achieve specific objectives and deliver memorable experiences for attendees. It involves coordinating various elements, logistics, and activities to ensure the successful execution of events, from conception to post-event evaluation. Here are key components and concepts of event planning and management:

1. Event Objectives and Goals : Event planning begins with defining clear objectives and goals to guide the planning process and measure the success of the event. Objectives may include raising awareness, generating leads, fostering relationships, celebrating milestones, or achieving specific outcomes.

2. Budgeting and Financial Management : Event planners create budgets and financial plans to allocate resources, estimate costs, and manage expenses throughout the planning and execution process. Budget considerations include venue rental, catering, audiovisual equipment, decorations, marketing, staffing, and contingencies.

3. Venue Selection and Logistics : Venue selection is a critical aspect of event planning, involving considerations such as location, capacity, accessibility, amenities, and ambiance. Event planners coordinate logistics such as venue setup, layout, seating arrangements, signage, parking, and transportation to ensure a seamless experience for attendees.

4. Event Marketing and Promotion : Event planners develop marketing and promotion strategies to attract attendees, generate interest, and drive registrations or ticket sales. Marketing tactics may include digital marketing, email campaigns, social media promotion, advertising, public relations, and partnerships with influencers or media outlets.

5. Program Development and Content Creation : Event planners design the event program, agenda, and content to engage attendees and deliver valuable experiences. They curate speakers, presentations, workshops, panels, entertainment, activities, and interactive elements to align with the event objectives and cater to the interests of the target audience.

6. Registration and Attendee Management : Event planners implement registration systems and processes to facilitate attendee registration, ticketing, and check-in. They manage attendee communications, provide event information, handle inquiries, and coordinate special accommodations or requirements for attendees.

7. Vendor and Supplier Coordination : Event planners work with vendors, suppliers, and service providers to secure necessary goods and services for the event. This includes catering, audiovisual production, equipment rentals, decor, entertainment, transportation, security, and staffing.

8. Risk Management and Contingency Planning : Event planners identify potential risks and develop contingency plans to mitigate unforeseen challenges or emergencies that may arise during the event. They assess risks related to safety, security, weather,

technical issues, cancellations, and other factors, and implement measures to address them.

9. On-Site Management and Execution : On the day of the event, event planners oversee all aspects of event execution, including setup, coordination of vendors and staff, attendee assistance, program management, and troubleshooting. They ensure that the event runs smoothly, according to plan, and that attendees have a positive experience.

10. Post-Event Evaluation and Analysis : After the event, event planners conduct post-event evaluation and analysis to assess the success of the event, gather feedback from attendees, and identify areas for improvement. They measure key performance indicators (KPIs), analyze data, and generate reports to inform future event planning efforts.

By effectively planning and managing events, event planners create memorable experiences, achieve organizational objectives, and build relationships with attendees, stakeholders, and partners. Event planning requires attention to detail, strong organizational skills, creativity, flexibility, and the ability to adapt to changing circumstances to ensure the success of events of all sizes and types.

Ideas for Study Material/Resources:
Books: "The Complete Guide to Successful Event Planning" by Shannon Kilkenny, "Event Planning: The Ultimate Guide to Successful Meetings, Corporate Events, Fundraising Galas, Conferences, Conventions, Incentives and Other Special Events" by Judy Allen, "The Business of Event Planning: Behind-the-Scenes Secrets of Successful Special Events" by Judy Allen and Gary Yukl.
Online Courses: Platforms like Coursera, Udemy, and Eventbrite offer courses on event planning and management, covering topics such as event design, budgeting, marketing, and logistics.
Industry Associations: Organizations like the International Live Events Association (ILEA) and Meeting Professionals International (MPI) provide resources, webinars, and networking opportunities for event professionals.

Ideas for Activity:
Assign event planning projects where participants plan and execute mock events, including developing event concepts, creating budgets, sourcing vendors, and coordinating logistics.
Organize event simulation exercises or role-playing scenarios where participants work together to solve event-related challenges, such as last-minute changes or unexpected emergencies.

Some Training Ideas for Facilitation:
Start by introducing participants to the fundamentals of event planning and management, including the event planning process, key roles and responsibilities, and common challenges.

Provide an overview of event planning tools and techniques, such as event timelines, budget templates, venue selection criteria, vendor contracts, and risk management strategies.

Demonstrate how to plan and execute various types of events, from small meetings and conferences to large-scale festivals and conventions, covering aspects such as theme development, marketing and promotion, attendee engagement, and post-event evaluation.

Did You Know?
Event planning is ranked among the most stressful professions, alongside military personnel and firefighters, according to a survey by CareerCast.

The global events industry generates billions of dollars in economic impact annually and employs millions of people worldwide across various sectors, including hospitality, tourism, entertainment, and marketing.

Ideas for Presentation:
Create a PowerPoint presentation or e-book summarizing key event planning concepts, strategies, and best practices. Include templates, checklists, and case studies to help participants plan and execute successful events.

Training Video Guide:
Develop video tutorials or event planning training videos demonstrating key event planning and management concepts and techniques. Cover topics such as venue selection, budgeting, marketing, logistics, and on-site coordination. Use real-life examples and case studies to illustrate effective event planning practices.

Skills 69: Training Methods / Presentation Tools

Importance:
Training methods and presentation tools are essential for delivering engaging and effective learning experiences to learners and audiences. Proficiency in training methods and presentation tools enables trainers, educators, and presenters to communicate information clearly, facilitate learning, and enhance audience engagement.

Concept:
Training methods encompass a variety of techniques and strategies for delivering instruction, including lectures, discussions, hands-on activities, simulations, and multimedia presentations. Presentation tools refer to software applications and technologies used to create and deliver visual presentations, such as slideshows, videos, and interactive content.

Takeaway: Guide for Students and Professionals
By mastering training methods and presentation tools, individuals can design and deliver dynamic training sessions, lectures, and presentations that captivate audiences, reinforce learning, and achieve learning objectives. Proficiency in training

methods and presentation tools is valuable for educators, trainers, public speakers, and anyone involved in knowledge dissemination.

Training methods and presentation tools are essential components of effective learning and development initiatives, enabling trainers and presenters to deliver engaging and impactful training sessions to learners. Here are key components and concepts of training methods and presentation tools:

Training Methods:

1. Lecture : Lecture-based training involves the delivery of information, concepts, and content by an instructor or subject matter expert to learners through verbal presentation. Lectures may include slides, visuals, demonstrations, or storytelling to convey information and engage learners.

2. Hands-On Training : Hands-on training, also known as experiential learning or interactive learning, allows learners to actively engage in learning activities, exercises, simulations, or practical tasks related to the subject matter. Hands-on training promotes active learning, skill development, and retention through direct experience and application.

3. Group Discussion : Group discussion involves facilitated discussions among learners to explore ideas, share perspectives, and exchange knowledge and experiences related to the training topic. Group discussions promote collaboration, critical thinking, and peer learning, allowing participants to learn from each other's insights and viewpoints.

4. Role-Playing : Role-playing exercises allow learners to simulate real-life scenarios, interactions, or situations relevant to the training topic. Participants assume different roles or personas and engage in role-play activities to practice skills, behaviors, and communication techniques in a safe and supportive environment.

5. Case Studies : Case studies are real-world examples or scenarios that illustrate key concepts, principles, or best practices related to the training topic. Learners analyze case studies, identify issues, and propose solutions or recommendations based on their understanding and application of the subject matter.

6. e-Learning and Online Training : e-Learning and online training involve the delivery of training content and materials through digital platforms, learning management systems (LMS), or online courses. e-Learning enables learners to access training materials anytime, anywhere, and engage in self-paced learning activities, interactive modules, quizzes, and assessments.

7. Blended Learning : Blended learning combines traditional face-to-face instruction with online learning components to create a hybrid training experience. Blended learning programs may include a mix of classroom sessions, e-learning modules, virtual instructor-led training (VILT), and hands-on activities to accommodate diverse learning preferences and needs.

8. Microlearning : Microlearning involves delivering short, focused learning units or modules that are concise, targeted, and easily digestible. Microlearning modules are

typically brief, ranging from a few minutes to 10-15 minutes in duration, and focus on specific topics, tasks, or learning objectives.

9. On-the-Job Training (OJT) : On-the-job training involves learning and skill development that occurs within the context of the workplace environment. OJT allows learners to acquire knowledge and skills through observation, shadowing, mentoring, coaching, and hands-on experience under the guidance of experienced colleagues or supervisors.

10. Gamification : Gamification applies game elements, mechanics, and principles to training activities to increase engagement, motivation, and learning retention. Gamified training may include quizzes, challenges, rewards, badges, leaderboards, and interactive simulations to make learning more enjoyable and immersive.

Presentation Tools:
1. Presentation Software : Presentation software, such as Microsoft PowerPoint, Google Slides, or Apple Keynote, allows presenters to create and deliver visually engaging slide presentations. Presentation tools offer features for creating slides, adding text, images, graphics, animations, and multimedia elements, and customizing slide layouts and designs.

2. Interactive Whiteboards : Interactive whiteboards are digital display screens or boards that allow presenters to interact with content using touch, stylus, or digital pen input. Interactive whiteboards enable presenters to annotate, draw, highlight, and manipulate content in real-time during presentations or training sessions.

3. Video Conferencing Tools : Video conferencing tools, such as Zoom, Microsoft Teams, or Webex, enable presenters to conduct virtual presentations, webinars, or training sessions with remote participants. Video conferencing tools offer features for screen sharing, video streaming, chat, polling, and audience engagement to facilitate interactive and collaborative presentations.

4. Document Cameras : Document cameras, also known as visualizers or document scanners, capture and display physical documents, objects, or materials in real-time during presentations or training sessions. Presenters can use document cameras to showcase documents, illustrations, demonstrations, or hands-on activities to enhance visual communication and engagement.

5. Audience Response Systems (ARS) : Audience response systems, also known as clickers or polling tools, enable presenters to interact with audiences and gather real-time feedback, opinions, or responses during presentations or training sessions. ARS allows participants to respond to questions, quizzes, or surveys using mobile devices or handheld clickers, and view aggregated results instantly.

6. Screen Recording and Capture Tools : Screen recording and capture tools allow presenters to record, capture, and share video recordings or screenshots of presentations, demonstrations, or software applications. Screen recording tools

enable presenters to create tutorials, training videos, or screencasts for on-demand viewing or asynchronous learning.

7. Virtual Reality (VR) and Augmented Reality (AR) : Virtual reality (VR) and augmented reality (AR) technologies enable presenters to create immersive and interactive presentations or training experiences. VR and AR tools allow users to visualize and interact with 3D models, simulations, or virtual environments to enhance learning, engagement, and retention.

8. Webinar Platforms : Webinar platforms are specialized software platforms designed for hosting and delivering webinars, online presentations, or virtual events to remote audiences. Webinar platforms offer features for registration, hosting, audience engagement, chat, Q&A, and analytics to facilitate interactive and engaging presentations.

9. Learning Management Systems (LMS) : Learning management systems (LMS) allow presenters to deliver and manage training content, courses, and materials in an online learning environment. LMS platforms offer features for uploading, organizing, tracking, and delivering presentations, videos, documents, quizzes, and assessments to learners.

10. Mobile Apps and Tablets : Mobile apps and tablets provide portable and interactive presentation tools for presenters to deliver content, engage audiences, and facilitate collaboration. Presenters can use mobile apps and tablets to access presentation software, annotate slides, control presentations remotely, and interact with audiences in real-time.

By leveraging a variety of training methods and presentation tools, trainers, educators, and presenters can create dynamic, engaging, and effective learning experiences that cater to diverse learning styles, preferences, and needs. Whether delivering in-person, online, or hybrid training sessions, the right combination of training methods and presentation tools can enhance learner engagement, retention, and overall training effectiveness.

Ideas for Study Material/Resources:
Books: "The Trainer's Handbook: The AMA Guide to Effective Training" by Karen Lawson, "Presentation Zen: Simple Ideas on Presentation Design and Delivery" by Garr Reynolds, "Training for Dummies" by Elaine Biech.
Online Courses: Platforms like Coursera, Udemy, and LinkedIn Learning offer courses on training methods, presentation skills, and popular presentation tools such as PowerPoint, Prezi, and Google Slides.
Presentation Tools: Explore tutorials, guides, and user manuals provided by presentation tool vendors, such as Microsoft Office support for PowerPoint, Prezi tutorials, and Google Slides Help Center.

Ideas for Activity:
Conduct presentation design workshops where participants create engaging slideshows or multimedia presentations using various presentation tools.

Organize training method demonstrations or role-playing exercises where participants practice delivering training sessions using different instructional techniques, such as lectures, group discussions, and hands-on activities.

Some Training Ideas for Facilitation:
Start by introducing participants to the principles of effective training and presentation design, including audience analysis, learning objectives, content organization, and engagement strategies.
Provide an overview of different training methods and presentation techniques, such as active learning, storytelling, visual aids, and interactive media.
Demonstrate how to use popular presentation tools effectively, including tips for creating visually appealing slides, incorporating multimedia elements, and delivering presentations confidently.

Did You Know?
According to research, visuals in presentations improve comprehension and retention by up to 400% compared to text-only presentations.
The use of interactive elements such as quizzes, polls, and Q&A sessions can significantly enhance audience engagement and participation during presentations and training sessions.

Ideas for Presentation:
Create a PowerPoint presentation or e-book summarizing key training methods, presentation design principles, and best practices. Include examples, templates, and case studies to guide participants in creating effective presentations and training materials.

Training Video Guide:
Develop video tutorials or training method/presentation tool training videos demonstrating how to use popular presentation tools and implement effective training methods. Cover topics such as slide design, storytelling, audience engagement techniques, and interactive presentation features.

Appendix

Resource E-Book World @ SkillUp Store
(Drive Resource)